# JEREMIAH
## THROUGH
# DANIEL

## WESLEY BIBLE STUDIES

**wesleyan**
PUBLISHING HOUSE
wphstore.com

Copyright © 2015 by Wesleyan Publishing House
Published by Wesleyan Publishing House
Indianapolis, Indiana 46250
Printed in the United States of America
ISBN: 978-0-89827-868-2
ISBN (e-book): 978-0-89827-869-9

# CONTENTS

Introduction    5

1. Power in the Spirit
Jeremiah 31:31–34; Ezekiel 36:25–27    8

2. The Reason for Our Confidence
Jeremiah 17:5–14    16

3. Clay in the Potter's Hands
Jeremiah 18:1–10    25

4. Seeing God at Work
Jeremiah 29:10–14; 32:6–15, 36–44    34

5. Experiencing God's Discipline
Lamentations 3:19–40    43

6. When God Speaks
Ezekiel 1:1, 25–28; 2:1–8    52

7. Repent and Live!
Ezekiel 18:20–32    61

8. Experiencing God's Compassion
Ezekiel 34:7–16; Jeremiah 23:1–6    70

9. New Hope
Ezekiel 37:1–14    79

10. The Power of Integrity
Daniel 1:8–20    88

11. Learning to Trust God
Daniel 3:1, 4–6, 12–28    97

12. From Pride to Humility
Daniel 4:28–37    105

13. Enduring Conflict Faithfully
Daniel 6:10–23    114

Words from Wesley Works Cited    123

# INTRODUCTION

*The Way Forward*

---

It was a dark period in the history of God's people. Not since the time of the judges had the nation faced such peril both from external enemies and unfaithfulness within. In spite of repeated calls for repentance by the prophets, and at least one attempt at reform, God's people remained on a course for destruction. It came at the hands of the Assyrian Empire, which conquered the northern kingdom of Israel in 721 B.C., and the Babylonian Empire, which finally subdued the southern kingdom of Judah in 587 B.C., deporting a large number of Jews to Babylon.

What next? How would God's people respond to His judgment? What hope could there be after so great a catastrophe as the siege of Jerusalem and the destruction of God's temple? The writings of three prophets—Jeremiah, Ezekiel, and Daniel—point the way forward.

## JEREMIAH: GOD DISCIPLINES AND COMFORTS

We begin with Jeremiah, the weeping prophet, who began his ministry in 628 B.C., only two decades before the destruction of his nation. Jeremiah was one of the few who foresaw the national disaster that lay just a few years beyond the horizon. He used enacted prophecies, what we now might call performance art, to illustrate the unfaithfulness of the nation and its impending judgment. His heart-rending prophecies went largely unheeded. Jeremiah was imprisoned by the leaders of his country, and he remained in captivity until the entire nation was taken captive in 587 B.C. by the Babylonians, who, ironically, freed Jeremiah.

Jeremiah's writing centers on the opposing themes of judgment and mercy. The sensitive prophet unflinchingly predicted God's judgment for sin, yet his lament for the city of Jerusalem also presents our most tender description of God's care for His people. Within Jeremiah's writing are the seeds of hope.

## EZEKIEL: GOD RESTORES

Ezekiel was one of the Israelites who was taken into exile, perhaps in the year 587 B.C. He wrote as a stranger in a strange land—a priest of the Lord forced to live far from his home and from the Lord's temple, which lay in ruins. His imaginative writing is rich with symbols, including the well-known valley of dry bones (Ezek. 37). Although this book contains many passages of judgment, Ezekiel also turned his prophetic eye toward the future, envisioning the grand way in which God would restore His people. In Ezekiel's writing, we are reminded of the connection between repentance and restoration. God's plan is ultimately about the future, not the past. When we repent, we live.

## DANIEL: GOD CAN BE TRUSTED

Daniel is one of the great heroes of the exilic period. Along with other Jewish young men, Daniel was carried into captivity in Babylon, probably with the first wave of deportation in 606 B.C. Yet Daniel's life was not all hardship. He and his three famous companions (Shadrach, Meshach, and Abednego) were placed in the service of the Babylonian king, where they faced a more subtle form of adversity—the pressure to conform to a worldly culture. Neither the temptations of court life nor the threat of execution could make Daniel surrender his integrity. Best known for his determined stand in the lions' den, Daniel exemplifies the faithful person's ability to live a life of holiness amid the most trying circumstances. From Daniel we learn the power of integrity, the importance of humility, and the certainty that God will stand with those who trust Him.

This study promises both challenge and comfort, and the firm confidence that God has your future under control.

# POWER IN THE SPIRIT

*Jeremiah 31:31–34; Ezekiel 36:25–27*

---

The Holy Spirit gives us the inner power to obey God consistently.

**W**hen a group of ministers wanted to call evangelist Dwight L. Moody to hold special services in their city, one of them objected. "All I hear about these days is D. L. Moody! Does Moody have a monopoly on the Holy Spirit?"

"No," answered another minister, "but the Holy Spirit has a monopoly on D. L. Moody!"

What does it mean for the Holy Spirit to have a monopoly on an individual? What would it take to live that kind of life? Is it for everyone?

This study shows why it is vital for Christians to submit themselves to the control of the Holy Spirit and the practical difference that will make in our ability to live consistently faithful lives.

## COMMENTARY

The New Testament gives a great deal of attention to the Spirit's work in the life of a believer, but the Holy Spirit was not unknown during Old Testament times, and His sanctifying work was eagerly anticipated by many of the prophets.

Jeremiah was one of them. He was a prophet to the kingdom of Judah during its last forty years of existence (627–586 B.C.). It was a turbulent time, witnessing a brief period of revival under King Josiah, but also the ultimate disintegration of the kingdom and the destruction of Jerusalem and the temple. Jeremiah spent his last years as an exile in Egypt. The book that bears his name is both an autobiography of the prophet as well as a biography of Judah. In it, history, prophecy, poetry, and confession combine to present God's message of doom for Jerusalem, and His word of hope in the gospel of the new covenant. Jeremiah looked forward to the day when God would restore His people.

Ezekiel was another of those prophets. He was raised in Jerusalem in a priestly home and was deported to Babylonia in 597 B.C. along with King Jehoiachin and many other citizens of Judah. Five years later, he received his call from the Lord to prophesy. Initially his message was directed toward Jerusalem with warnings and symbolic actions designed to bring Judah to repentance and to her historic faith in God. Then, after Jerusalem's destruction, he became a pastor to the exiles and a messenger of comfort and hope. He too looked forward to the day when God would restore the people to their land and give them a new heart that would follow Him.

Like Jeremiah and Ezekiel, Paul was also called by the Lord to be a prophet. But unlike them, Paul lived and ministered in the period of the new covenant. He actually experienced what Jeremiah and Ezekiel only hoped for and pointed to. He grew up as a devout Jew, receiving a thorough education in the Old Testament law. But until God met him on the road to Damascus, Paul's heart was still cold and sinful. Nevertheless, God's Spirit ultimately transformed him into a saint and an apostle to the Gentiles (Eph. 1:1). His letter to the Ephesians helps believers see both what they once were outside of Christ, as well as what they have now become through the sanctifying ministry of the Spirit.

## A New Covenant (Jer. 31:31–34)

Israel and Judah were in trouble. The northern kingdom of Israel had been defeated years before by Assyria and laid waste. Now Nebuchadnezzar, king of Babylon, had conquered the southern kingdom of Judah, deposed their king, and taken many of the leading citizens into exile. God had made a covenant with Israel at Mount Sinai that He would be their God, and they in turn would be His people. But Israel had forsaken the covenant and worshiped other gods instead. So now God was using the surrounding nations as His tool of discipline to bring them back to himself.

But Jeremiah told the people that a time was coming when God would once again be the God of all the clans of Israel, and they would be His people (31:1). Speaking for the Lord he said, **"The time is coming . . . when I will make a new covenant with the house of Israel and with the house of Judah"** (v. 31). This new covenant, God said, was to be different than the one He had previously made with their forefathers after bringing them out of slavery in Egypt. Jeremiah was the first of the prophets to use the phrase **new covenant**, but he was not the only one. They all looked forward to a new relationship with God and His people. And the New Testament writers all saw the fulfillment of this passage in the work of Jesus Christ (see, for example, Heb. 8:8–12; 10:16–17; Luke 22:20).

## WORDS FROM WESLEY

*Jeremiah 31:31*

It is not called the new covenant, because it was as to the substance new, for it was made with Abraham, Gen. 17:7, and with the Jews, Deut. 26:17, 18, but because it was revealed after a new manner, more fully and particularly, plainly and clearly. Nor was the ceremonial law any part of it, as it was to the Jews, a strict observance of that. It was likewise new in regard of the efficacy of the spirit attending it, in a much fuller and larger manner. (ENOT)

Since the people had been unable to keep the first covenant, the new covenant was to be a covenant of grace rather than works. The Lord says, **"I will make . . . I will put . . . I will be . . . I will forgive"** (Jer. 31:33–34). He himself takes the initiative. He only asks us to respond. One thing He says He will do is to **put** His **laws in their minds and write them on their hearts** (v. 33). The heart, in this context, was conceived as the seat of a person's will, intellect, and emotions. Previously, He had told the people that their sin was "engraved with an iron tool . . . on the tablets of their hearts" (17:1). In that condition, they could not help but sin. But apparently Jeremiah had in mind that God was able to erase what was there and replace it with His law so that God's people would naturally follow Him. Obedience would not be external to some code of law, but internal to the affection of their hearts.

---

### WORDS FROM WESLEY

*Jeremiah 31:33*

*With*—That is, with those who are Jews inwardly. *And write it*—The prophet's design is here to express the difference between the law and the gospel. The first shows duty, the latter brings the grace of regeneration, by which the heart is changed, and enabled for duty. All under the time of the law that came to salvation, were saved by this new covenant; but this was not evidently exhibited; neither was the regenerating grace of God so common under the time of the law, as it hath been under the gospel. (ENOT)

---

Another thing God says He will do is to **be their God, and they will be** His **people** (31:33). It will be a covenant of personal relationship. And it will also be a covenant of intimate knowledge— **They will all know me** (v. 34). This will be not merely a head knowledge of the facts, but a heart knowledge through personal experience, the kind Paul later expressed in 2 Timothy 1:12 when he said, "I know whom I have believed."

Finally, God says that in this new covenant He **will forgive their wickedness and will remember their sins no more** (v. 34). Under the old covenant, this was done temporarily through the sacrifice of animals by a priest in the temple. But under the new covenant, forgiveness would be complete because the sacrifice itself would be perfect—God's one and only Son offered as an atonement for sin on the altar of Calvary.

## A New Heart (Ezek. 36:25–27)

The nations of Israel and Judah lay in waste. Assyria had destroyed the northern kingdom of Israel in 722 B.C. Babylonia had laid waste to Judah in 586 B.C. Both were objects of God's punishment because of their sin. Ezekiel prophesied, "Son of man, when the people of Israel were living in their own land, they defiled it by their conduct and their actions. Their conduct was like a woman's monthly uncleanness in my sight. So I poured out my wrath on them because they had shed blood in the land and because they had defiled it with their idols. I dispersed them among the nations" (36:17–19). But God did not forget them or His covenant with them. He declared that He would eventually restore them and bring them back into their own land (v. 24). And this act would be rooted solely in God's divine grace, for the sake of His holy name (vv. 22–23). God's pure grace is manifested in a promise to His people.

In addition to restoring them to the land He had given their forefathers, the Lord also promised to change their hearts. He declared that He **will sprinkle clean water on** them, **and** they **will be clean** (v. 25). He had originally called them to be holy even as He was holy (Lev. 19:2). But they had become dirty as a result of their sin. The Old Testament law provided for various ceremonial washings when the people became "unclean" and were separated from the fellowship and the worship. But here the Lord declared that He himself would **cleanse** them **from all** their **impurities and from all** their **idols** (Ezek. 36:25). Idolatry over several hundred years had left a deep scar in the conscience of the people and had profaned even the land itself. But God was determined to cleanse even that ugly stain.

In addition to washing away the stains of their sin, the Lord also promised that He would **give** them **a new heart and put a new spirit in** them (v. 26). Merely being forgiven was not enough. They needed a new heart and a new spirit to replace the **heart of stone** that belonged to their old nature. It was defective because it had a continual pull toward sin. But God, through His grace, promised to replace it with **a heart of flesh**. This is truly the work of God in sanctification—to wash away the impurity caused by sin, and then enable one from within to live above it!

---

### WORDS FROM WESLEY
#### Ezekiel 36:26

*A new heart*—A new frame of soul, a mind changed, from sinful to holy, from carnal to spiritual. A heart in which the law of God is written, Jer. 31:33. A sanctified heart, in which the almighty grace of God is victorious, and turns it from all sin to God. *A new spirit*—A new, holy frame in the spirit of man; which is given to him, not wrought by his own power. *The stony*—The senseless unfeeling. *Out of your flesh*—Out of you. *Of flesh*—That is, quite of another temper, hearkening to God's law, trembling at His threats, moulded into a compliance with His whole will; to forbear, do, be, or suffer what God will, receiving the impress of God, as soft wax receives the impress of the seal. (ENOT)

---

And the way all this becomes possible is through the filling of the Holy Spirit. God said, **"I will put my Spirit in you and move you to follow my decrees"** (v. 27). Throughout the Old

Testament, God's Spirit came upon people in certain times and places to empower them to fulfill certain tasks. But here God's promise was that a time was coming when His Spirit would live in them, purifying their hearts and enabling them to walk in obedience to God's law. That day is here!

## DISCUSSION

Share your thoughts about an old saying which says that an organization should have as many rules as necessary but as few as possible.

1. The Israelites appeared religious, but they were often faithless. What issues caused them to fall into this cycle of disobedience?

2. Name some ways in which a stone heart is like the stony ground in Matthew 13:5.

3. In Ephesians 4, what did Paul mean by "put off your old self" and "put on the new self"? How much of that is God's work and how much is ours?

4. In what specific ways might the renewal of a person's mind be shown in his or her conduct?

5. Have you ever experienced a time when it was hard to do what you believed God (or Scripture) told you to do? What was it like?

6. What makes it so difficult to let go of old habits or thoughts?

7. If you were to do a spiritual housecleaning in your life, where would you begin?

8. If that cleaning required the Holy Spirit to have an all-access pass into your thoughts, heart, actions, and goals, which area would be the most difficult for you to surrender?

9. What direction would your life take if you renewed your relationship with God right now?

## PRAYER

Father, Your holiness stands in stark contrast to our righteousness. Enable us by Your Spirit to love You and become like You.

## 2

# THE REASON FOR OUR CONFIDENCE

*Jeremiah 17:5–14*

---

We live confidently because we rely on God
rather than our own resources.

Everybody puts faith in something. Whether it is modern medicine, science, political power, money, or something else, all of us rely on *something* as a source of comfort, security, and meaning. To find that object of belief, many people look no further than themselves. They rely on their own intellect, physical prowess, or intuition to make their lives secure and comfortable. That is a mistake many people fail to discover until some catastrophe comes.

Jeremiah wrote to a people who had come to rely on themselves for security, and his message applies equally well to us today—God is the only reliable object of our trust.

This study will lead you to have confidence for whatever you are facing in life by placing your trust in God alone.

## COMMENTARY

Beginning in 628 B.C., Jeremiah ministered to God's people for about thirty years. This was a period of national crisis, just before (and as) the nation of Judah was exiled to Babylon. (Assyria had conquered the northern kingdom of Israel a century before.) Then, when Babylon overtook Judah, Jeremiah joined a group trying to find refuge in Egypt. Tradition tells us he was stoned to death while in Egypt.

The format of the book of Jeremiah is argued to have an odd structure. The book appears as an anthology containing twenty or more separate sections, pasted together without apparent logical or chronological sequence. The outline lacks any overall pattern. No one knows when and under what circumstances this book assumed its present form. Baruch, Jeremiah's "secretary," may have compiled his master's ideas (see 45:1–2 for one mention of Baruch's service to Jeremiah).

What is Jeremiah's overall message? Five concepts summarize his preaching: (1) Judah has been unfaithful to God; (2) God does not tolerate such lack of respect; (3) Judah must repent; (4) if the nation continues on its present path, God will judge Judah; (5) God's people should focus their attention on Him, not on the national crisis.

Jeremiah 17:5–14 records a conversation between God and Jeremiah. Through the prophet, God gave Judah words of potential judgment and blessing, but Jeremiah interrupted with some thoughts of his own.

### God's First Statement (Jer. 17:5–8)

As Babylon threatened Judah, its king and people were tempted to seek protection not from God but from nearby nations, particularly Egypt. As people do today, the threatened Judeans preferred to depend on human help they could see (**flesh**, v. 5), rather than divine help not so easily seen. How silly! Egypt had recently proved to be no match for Babylon. God, who had revealed His power when He brought His people out of Egypt hundreds of years before, could perform national miracles once again.

**Cursed is the one who trusts in man** (v. 5). This verse in no way implies that God was looking for an excuse to dump His people. He merely stated the fact that those who depend on undependable help always end up short. As God spoke these words to and through Jeremiah, He was repeating the curses (and, later, in vv. 7–8, the blessings) He had already promised in Deuteronomy 27 and 28.

Jeremiah 17:6 repeats the content of verse 5 in picture form. The nation that turns from God, the true protector, to other nations finds itself as vulnerable as a **bush** in the desert. Consider all the factors going against bushes in the desert: They lack water (**parched**). They lack strong connections with the ground in which they live. (Contrast with the **roots** [v. 8] of trees in fertile wetlands.) They never grow tall. They live in a **land where no one lives**. (This implies not only solitude, but death. Nothing, not even bushes, can live in the desert for long.) This verse gives a vivid picture of the uncomfortable exile Judah faced.

**But** (v. 7). Here Jeremiah made the transition to a better way. God's word in verse 7 directly contrasts the content of verse 5. The contrast in these verses gives a strong picture of true belief. Biblical faith goes so far beyond merely giving mental assent to a fact. Picture yourself taking a poll in ancient Judea. You could ask all kinds of questions about the national deity and probably hear 100 percent correct answers. "How many gods are there? To what God does Judah swear allegiance?" The people of Judah knew their nation followed the one God of Abraham, Isaac, and Jacob. But how did that knowledge translate into military strategy? Jeremiah knew that far too many Judeans, no matter what they said they believed, would rather seek protection from Egypt than from God. Did these people believe in God? In one sense, yes. They could name Him as their God. But did they truly believe? Did they place their confidence in Him? No. (Before you condemn Judah for its weakness, make sure you draw all the appropriate comparisons to yourself, your church, and your nation.)

As verse 7 contrasts verse 5, so verse 8 offers a picture quite different from verse 6. Perhaps you can remember a childhood scene or a park you have visited that included a tall, old tree by a river. You sat in its shade, soaking in its green beauty. Jeremiah stated the ideal: deep roots, steady water supply (compare

Jeremiah's description in verse 13 of God as the "spring of living water"), annual bearing of fruit. If only Judah would truly depend on God, if only Judah would follow the ways of God, it too could enjoy a life much closer to paradise (see Deut. 28).

### Jeremiah Questioned God (Jer. 17:9)

As Jeremiah listened to himself speaking the words of God, he may have struggled on at least two counts.

First, in relation to the nation he loved, Jeremiah knew God's warning was accurate. He knew Judah's only way around tragedy was a return to God. But could God's people return to Him? Jeremiah saw little hope. Why? **The heart** (individually and nationally) **is deceitful above all things and beyond cure** (v. 9). "God, You may have been able to change the heart of our father Jacob, but things have gotten worse since then. God, it seems even You can't cleanse the black heart of Judah." Jeremiah, a true prophet, loved his people and cringed at the thought of their doom.

---

### WORDS FROM WESLEY

*Jeremiah 17:9*

*The heart*—There is nothing so false and deceitful as the heart of man; deceitful in its apprehensions of things, in the hopes and promises which it nourishes, in the assurances that it gives us; unsearchable by others, deceitful with reference to ourselves, and abominably wicked, so that neither can a man know his own heart, nor can any other know that of his neighbor's. (ENOT)

---

Second, Jeremiah may have struggled to accept the words God had spoken through him. "God, You promised that the man who depended on You would flourish. By faithfully proclaiming the hard words You have given me, I have shown my true dependence on You. Why am I suffering so much? **Who can understand it?**" (v. 9). If you don't think a hero such as Jeremiah could think such thoughts, see 15:17–18, where he spoke almost those exact words. In those verses, Jeremiah even used the water image, pointing out that God's promised supply appeared to be drying up. On that day, as Jeremiah took his doubts to God, God had reassured Jeremiah that He would keep His covenantal promise. But perhaps, as he spoke the words recorded in chapter 17, Jeremiah continued to wonder.

## God Replied (Jer. 17:10–11)

God basically informed Jeremiah that He remains in control: "Jeremiah, you think you have the situation figured out. But I still know a bit more than you do. **I** (not you, Jeremiah) **. . . search the heart and examine the mind** (v. 10). Jeremiah, I know the purity of *your* heart. I also know the black heart of the nation. I offer the possibility of repentance, but I still must judge those who have turned from Me."

## WORDS FROM WESLEY

*Jeremiah 17:9*

O my false, deceitful heart,
Desperately false thou art,
Foul as hell, when fair in show;
Who can all the mazes know?
He the stars may reckon o'er,
Tell the sands that bound the shore,
Count the drops that make the sea,
Comprehend eternity.
Foolish heart, unjust and vain!
Pride was never made for man;
Glory dost thou still pursue;
Glory all to God is due.
What hast thou whereof to boast?
God alone is good and just;
Only His be all the praise;
What we are, we are by grace.
Wretched heart, with woes opprest!
Ever roving after rest:
Wilt thou still pretend to own
Bliss is found in God alone?
While thy foolish wishes go
After empty joys below,
False imaginary ease,
Dreams of creature happiness.
Stony heart, which nought can move!
Thou canst neither fear nor love:
Threats and promises are vain,
Give thee neither joy nor pain:
All alike, it seems, to thee
Perfect bliss or misery,
Joys or woes unspeakable,
Life or death, and heaven or hell.
O my Lord, what must I do?
Only Thou the way canst show,
Thou canst save me in this hour,
I have neither will nor power:
God if over all Thou art,
Greater than the sinful heart,
Let it now on me be shown,
Take away the heart of stone. (PW, vol. 2, 86–89)

God promised **to reward** people (Jeremiah and Judah) **according to** their **conduct,** their **deeds** (v. 10). We of the New Testament era find those words a bit difficult to swallow. "That sounds like works-righteousness. Where's God's grace?" we may ask. The simple answer we often give to such questions revolves around the truth that God is more concerned with hearts than with actions. Thus we emphatically state that God wants to transform people on the inside so they can do that which pleases God. There's truth there, but we need to remember the foundational fact that God feels grief over *both* sinful hearts and sinful actions. He feels concern over both **heart** and **conduct**; He wishes to transform both **mind** and **deeds**.

What about the concept of reward? Can human beings earn God's love? No. He gives His love freely. But that does not deny the fact that He enjoys blessing those who do what is right.

The next verse describes one god not worthy of trust: wealth. People with deceitful hearts often worship this god, to the extent of seeking more money even if they have to steal it (**gain**[ing] **riches by unjust means,** v. 11). Again God and Jeremiah combine to offer a priceless picture of this person: **a partridge that hatches eggs it did not lay**. **When his** (the surrogate mother or the greedy man) **life is half gone, they** (the adopted animal children or the ill-gotten wealth) **will desert him**. Again God stated the basic fact that the person who depends on the undependable ends up looking like a **fool.**

### Jeremiah Reflected (Jer. 17:12–14)

Jeremiah, at this point, chose to speak once again—this time not with doubt but with trust. These next three verses begin and end with praise for God. In verse 12, Jeremiah affirmed the value of the temple. He did so, not to glorify the building itself, but because the temple served as the dwelling place for the **throne** of the God who would prove himself faithful. This passage ends with straightforward worship: **You are the one I praise** (v. 14).

Verse 13 offers Jeremiah's affirmation of the truth God has spoken through him to the nation. God through Jeremiah had condemned those who do not trust in God (vv. 5–6, 11). Here Jeremiah, speaking not to the nation but to God, stated his agreement: **All who forsake you will be put to shame** (v. 13).

Despite his faith in God, Jeremiah still felt some concern for his future, but he knew to whom he could take his fears: the God who heard his prayers: "If I ask You to **heal me**, **I will be healed**; if I ask You to **save me**, You will keep me safe" (v. 14). That God was and is certainly worthy of praise.

---

### WORDS FROM WESLEY
*Jeremiah 17:14*

*For thou art*—He whom alone I have reason to praise for mercies already received. (ENOT)

---

## DISCUSSION

Share about the last time you learned something new about yourself. Share what person or circumstance helped you to see it and if it was a good experience or a bad one.

1. What contrasts do you find in the passage that picture a "cursed" versus a "blessed" person?

2. What factors gave Jeremiah the strength to continue as a prophet through both the highs and lows of ministry?

3. Why do you think God is so concerned with the condition of our hearts and not merely with our good behavior?

4. Give some specific examples of how a person might place confidence in people rather than God.

5. Why do you think people turn to God more readily in crisis situations?

6. If it is futile to attempt to hide ourselves from God, why do we so often do it?

7. Water is vital for healthy plant life. What would be a comparable ingredient for a healthy spiritual life?

8. In what ways do your spiritual roots sustain you during tough times?

9. God sees your heart. Share one reason that statement gives you confidence.

## PRAYER

Heal us, O Lord, and we will be healed. Save us and we will be saved. You are the one we praise . . . always (see Jer. 17:14).

# 3

# CLAY IN THE POTTER'S HANDS

*Jeremiah 18:1–10*

God shapes the course of our lives as we submit to Him.

"Where is my life headed?" "What's my purpose?" "What legacy will I leave behind?"

Everyone asks questions like these at some point. Sooner or later, we all must grapple with the big question: "Why am I here?"

Compounding our difficulty in answering those questions are the failures we often experience. When life doesn't turn out the way we expected, the need for direction and purpose becomes even more urgent.

This study will help you realize that your true calling is to love and serve God. As you do, He will shape—and reshape—your life into a thing of beauty and purpose.

## COMMENTARY

The Hebrew word for *potter* means to "make" or "fashion." The earliest potters created vessels of stone. No one is quite sure when the shift from pottery of stone to ceramic vessels took place. But clay figurines were being fired in Syria and Palestine by the end of the seventh millennium. Once the art of making pottery from clay was discovered, artisans were quick to learn burnishing and painting skills. There was a great demand for pottery since it had great advantages over baskets, which would have been their only other containers. Obviously pottery was better for liquids or keeping grain safe from rodents.

To make the best pottery, the clay percentages needed to be just right. Clay that was too pure wasn't elastic enough. A ratio of about 50 percent clay to earth was needed to produce the best clay. The clay had to be taken from the earth and washed before it was ready for use.

Early pottery making was hard work since it was done all by hand. Later came the method of putting coils of clay on a wheel and smoothing them as the piece formed. Some pottery was made in a press mold. As it dried, it shrank and allowed for removal from the mold.

Several scriptural references in the Old Testament describe the process of pottery making. First Chronicles 4:23 speaks of those who were potters for the king (see also Ps. 2:9; Isa. 29:16; Lam. 4:2; and Zech. 11:13).

This passage in Jeremiah refers to the potter's house, which was usually near a field that was a good source of clay. This was not the potter's home, but his workshop. It would contain a kiln as well as the wheels for formation and a dump for broken pieces of pottery. The house would be little more than a hut with cover from the weather.

The wheel itself was usually an arrangement of two stone discs. The heavier one below gave momentum to keep the lighter (upper) disc turning, but the vessel was shaped on the upper disc. The potter's foot propelled the lower wheel, which was connected by a shaft that kept the upper wheel turning.

To prepare the clay, the potter kneaded it with his feet (see Nah. 3:14; Isa. 41:25). Next it was washed and then placed on the wheel, where the fingers of the potter determined the quality as well as the shape of the pottery. If the clay was not treated properly or washed sufficiently, the piece would not yield the potter's desired image. In this case, the piece could be crumpled into a ball and the reshaping process begun again. If the clay "refused" to form properly for whatever reason, it was cast aside.

(It was this process that Jeremiah was sent by God to watch and see the obvious analogies to the Israelites.)

The final product is determined by the firing. Skill is as critical here as in the throwing. However, no references in the Old Testament inform us as to the ancient techniques. There is a reference to the "Potsherd Gate," which is where misfired and broken pieces were dumped. There must have been quite a heap to name the city gate after a pile of broken pottery.

Pottery could be decorated in various ways. The most common technique was to impress a pattern on the wet clay by combings, incisions, or beading. Pottery was as essential to life then as now, and the variety of quality and style was great even then. Often in Scripture God uses the everyday things to illustrate theological truth. Jeremiah 18 is perhaps the best-known passage in the book and the saddest message—that of the uselessness of the Israelites due to their sins.

Having looked at the process of pottery making should enable us to better understand the analogy in this passage. Jeremiah 18 is perhaps the clearest statement in the Old Testament of the conditional nature of prophecy and God's promises: God's covenant with the Israelites was totally dependent on their obedience to it. To receive God's covenant promises, they had to obey the Law— the most important part of which was to worship *only* Yahweh. God, because He is holy, could not overlook their idolatry and let the promises "slide." The people of Israel never realized some of the promises because they could not bring themselves to worship *only* Jehovah God. This passage highlights how their sinfulness marred the "masterpiece" God had intended to make of them to set before the other nations. Now God had to reshape or throw away the piece. This is the unhappy message Jeremiah had deliver to them.

## The Purpose of Prophecy and the Obedience of the Prophet (Jer. 18:1–2)

**This is the word that came to Jeremiah from the LORD** (v. 1). The prophet's "job" was to speak the word of the Lord. He or she had no choice—either in *whether* to speak or *what* the message would be. God used the prophets as His own mouth. When He had something to say, He put the words into the mouths of His chosen speakers.

God used prophecy in at least six different ways.

One way God used prophecy was to rebuke. More than half of the prophecies in the Old Testament are in this category. The purpose is always to rebuke sin and call to repentance.

Revelation of facts about God and His creation was another purpose of prophecy. Interestingly, the seemingly most important facts about God and His character are usually imbedded in the messages of rebuke or encouragement. The totality of the prophecies provides a huge resource of knowledge of God and creation, but this information rarely stands alone.

Prophecy encouraged God's people. Although fewer in number than passages of rebuke, messages of encouragement were an essential part of the prophet's work. And they usually appear immediately after a rebuke. Sometimes the transition from rebuke seems so abrupt that it is hard to change focus that quickly, especially in Isaiah, Jeremiah, and Micah (compare Isa. 4:1 to 4:2–6).

God used prophecy to inform the people of action to be taken on a specific occasion. This comprises a small part of the prophet's total message, but was important to those first hearing the messages. An example is the directions frequently given to Moses and the people during their journeying.

Through the prophet's voice, God validated the authenticity of a divinely appointed leader or prophet. An example of this process is found when Samuel is told to anoint Saul as king of Israel.

Prophecies of the future Messiah was a sixth purpose of prophecy. These prophecies are also found imbedded in the current events of the people. They do not occur as "announcements" outside the context of a historical situation. For example, when Ahaz proved an unworthy head of the nation, Isaiah prophesied of a better "king" to come in the future (see Isa. 7:14). Because these prophecies also related to future events, the prophets often did not understand fully the messages they spoke. How could Isaiah have conceived that God would come in person to be head of His church?

**"Go . . . and there I will give you my message"** (v. 2). Even the prophet had to obey God's specific instructions. Jeremiah had to go to a certain place to receive God's message. In this case, the object lesson was for Jeremiah too. He needed to see the lesson of the potter to imprint it on his own heart and mind to better deliver it to the people.

---

### WORDS FROM WESLEY

*Jeremiah 18:2*

And thus it behooves every disciple of Christ to take up, as well as to bear, his cross. Indeed, in one sense, it is not his alone; it is common to him, and many others; seeing there is no temptation befalls any man . . . "but such as is common to men"; such as is incident and adapted to their common nature and situation in the present world. But, in another sense, as it is considered with all its circumstances, it is his; peculiar to himself: It is prepared of God for him; it is given by God to him, as a token of His love. And if he receives it as such, and, after using such means to remove the pressure as Christian wisdom directs, lies as clay in the potter's hand; it is disposed and ordered by God for His good, both with regard to the quality of it, and in respect to its quantity and degree, its duration, and every other circumstance. (WJW, vol. 6, 109)

### Picture of the Potter at Work (Jer. 18:3–4)

Jeremiah **went** to the place and **saw him working at the wheel** (v. 3). Just as Jeremiah could see the potter working, making something out of the clay, first Jeremiah and then the people were to understand that God was working to make something out of them. God had wanted them to be His missionaries to the rest of the world. God had meant to make them a beautiful "vessel" to hold His presence and display His glory to the nations around them.

The potter saw that his pot was **marred** (v. 4). This word for *marred* in Hebrew has rich meaning for the analogy being presented here. It basically means decayed, destroyed, or ruined. But it also carries a connotation of acting perversely or wickedly and destroying. This aptly describes the actions of the Israelites, who had acted wickedly and thus ruined what God was trying to fashion of them.

**So the potter formed . . . another pot, shaping it as seemed best to him** (v. 4). Neither God nor the potter can abide a marred pot. Just as the potter would crumple the clay into a ball and shape a new pot, so God was attempting to reshape the sinful Israelites into a new pot to better represent himself. What seemed best to Him was not what Israel expected—exile in a foreign country. But God was using adversity and exile to make them appreciate what they could have—a land of their own and all the prosperity promised in the covenant—if only they would obey Him.

### God's Message to Jeremiah and the People (Jer. 18:5–10)

**Then the word of the LORD came to me** (v. 5). The word came to Jeremiah *after* he obeyed and went to the potter's house, where God had a visible message awaiting him. Would the message have been given had Jeremiah not obeyed? Not with this vividness and force.

**"Can I not do with you as this potter does?"** (v. 6). The issue of God's ownership as Creator is heard in these verses. Just as the potter has absolute control over the clay and what he makes with it, so God holds sovereign power over the earth and all the people He has made. He can do whatever He likes with the people of Israel—first because they are His creation, and second because the covenant they have broken is His. He can destroy what they have become and reshape them any way He wishes. He does so not out of malice, but from a desire to redeem them (and the mess they have made).

---

### WORDS FROM WESLEY

*Jeremiah 18:6*

*Cannot I do*—God hath an absolute sovereign power to do what He pleases with the work of His hands: but He acts as a just judge, rendering to every man according to his works. (ENOT)

---

**"If . . . I announce that a nation or kingdom is to be uprooted"** (v. 7). God's control over the earth is absolute. Whether or not we see it, He causes nations to prosper or to be destroyed. But His control is rooted in goodness. There is no "playing chess" with the world or with His people. In the Old Testament, nations are blessed if they worship God and destroyed if they do not, and particularly if they try to harm God's chosen people. So we never fear God's actions being capricious or unjust. He acts in accordance with His nature and the laws He has communicated to us.

The Lord continued: **"If that nation I warned repents of its evil, then I will relent"** (v. 8). God never judges without warning. The people of Israel had been repeatedly warned through God's prophets. Also remember in the book of Jonah that God was set to destroy the people of Nineveh, but first sent Jonah with the message of repentance. When they repented, God did not punish them. God delights in repentance, not judgment.

**"If . . . I announce that a nation or kingdom is to be built up . . . and if it does evil in my sight and does not obey me"** (vv. 9–10). This emphasizes clearly the free will given to us. We can choose to obey and be blessed, or we can choose to do evil in God's sight and reap the punishment God has promised. God does not tolerate sin—even in His chosen people.

---

### WORDS FROM WESLEY

*Jeremiah 18:10*

The spirit of God directs all the creatures, upper and lower, so that they shall serve the divine purpose. Events are not determined by the wheel of fortune, which is blind, but by the wheels of providence, which are full of eyes. (ENOT, Ezek. 10:17)

## DISCUSSION

Share about an experience you've had on a team, either one that functioned well or poorly and what it was like.

1. Retell the incident at the potter's house in your own words.

2. What might the defect in the clay have represented in the life of ancient Israel?

3. What might a defect represent today in the life of a church or an individual?

4. Why isn't perfection our goal?

5. In what way do you see God's judgment at work in this story? In what way do you see His grace displayed?

6. Why do you think we are so often blind to our own faults and yet so aware of others'?

7. Share a time someone pointed out a fault of yours, and you were grateful.

8. If you were a clay creation, would you be more like a coffee mug or a flower vase? Why do you think so? Why do you think God created you as He did?

9. What factors might affect the way you see your purpose versus the way God views it?

10. Has your life ever been reshaped by God? Share that experience with the group.

## PRAYER

Melt, mold, fill, and use us, Lord.

# 4

# SEEING GOD AT WORK

*Jeremiah 29:10–14; 32:6–15, 36–44*

God desires the best for you!

It doesn't take long to get discouraged when listening to a news broadcast—all the news seems to be bad! Hearing of tough economic times, violence in our cities, sagging educational scores, and wars in various parts of the world can make us wonder, "Who is in control of this world anyway?" Add to that the difficult personal circumstances we sometimes face, such as illness, stress at work, or family problems, and we can easily lose hope in the future.

This study brings good news to people facing tough times. Jeremiah's hopeful words, given at a time when the outlook was bleaker than ever, will remind us that God is always in control and has a bright plan for our future.

## COMMENTARY

Jeremiah 29 was written after the second deportation in 597 B.C. and before the destruction of Jerusalem in 586.

The exiles in Babylonia hoped to return to their homeland soon, yet Jeremiah's prophetic messages gave no such hope. Rather, he spoke of the culmination of God's judgment against His people. And this letter was intended to counter the attitude that the return from exile was imminent.

Jeremiah 32 divides into four major sections: background information (vv. 1–5); report of the sign-act (vv. 6–15); Jeremiah's inquiring prayer (vv. 16–25); and God's response to the issues raised by Jeremiah's prayer (vv. 26–44).

## God's Specific Plans of Future Restoration (Jer. 29:10–14)

God promised two things to the people for the future: (1) His renewed presence with the people, and (2) a return from exile. These two promises are stated both at the beginning and the end of the paragraph.

There is an implied sequential relationship between those two items: *when* I come to you and am found by you, *then* I will return you to the land.

**"I will be found by you"** implies that God will be sought. See verses 12–13.

Verse 12 begins with **then**, which ties back to the time reference in verse 10: **when seventy years are completed . . . then**. So according to verses 10–14, when the seventy years of exile are finished, three related things happen: (1) People seek God; (2) God renews His presence; (3) God restores the people to the land. Thus verses 12–13 indicate that the precondition for reversing the situation of exile is the people's returning to God.

## God's General Declared Intent (Jer. 29:11)

Verse 11 provides assurance that God will bring about these plans because they are part of His intent toward His people: **For I know the plans I have for you . . . plans to prosper you and not to harm you, plans to give you hope and a future."** God purposes peace for His people (the literal reading here and in verse 7 of "prosperity"), which means more than just material blessings, but a condition of well-being and wholeness, and especially a sense of security.

Several things must be noted about the divine intent expressed in this verse. First, it is an intention for the "community" in that the **you** is plural not singular. In other words, God expresses here His intent for His people as a corporate entity, not necessarily as individuals.

Second, the complete fulfillment of those promises will occur in the future. The current generation will not experience the fulfillment of the promises, since they will occur *only* when the seventy years are completed. The outworking of God's plan expressed here will only be realized by future generations.

Third, there is a contingency. Although verse 11 expresses divine intent, the verses that follow imply there must be a human turning to God to fully appropriate the hope and future God intends for His people.

Fourth, God also announces "plans" for the community of God's people in Judah who refuse to listen to God's word (vv. 16–19). Those plans are not plans for peace, and they do not ring with hope for a bright future. In other words, the promise in verse 11 cannot be applied to every situation. Although God always desires to do good to us, there are also specific situations where, due to our sin, God decrees for us discipline and suffering.

Fifth, verse 11 is spoken to a people who were currently experiencing judgment, the exile. So the divine intent in verse 11 does not preclude judgment from happening. Rather, it promises judgment is not God's final word.

---

### WORDS FROM WESLEY

*Jeremiah 29:11*

*To give*—This deliverance will not depend upon your merits, but upon my own mercy, and kind thoughts and purposes I have for the seed of Abraham my servant, and I am resolved in my own thoughts what to do, I intend not the blotting out of the name of Israel from the earth, but to give such an end to their trouble as themselves expect and desire. (ENOT)

---

Given the context of verse 11, we must be cautious about glibly quoting it as if it means God will bring prosperity to us as individuals, never letting harm or judgment come to us. But it does provide an ultimate sense of hope. Even though we, individually and corporately, might be suffering and might experience the discipline of God, such is not God's ultimate plan for His people, the church.

## Sign-Act of Purchasing the Field (Jer. 32:6–15)

Verses 6–15 are the report of a "sign-act." A sign-act is an object lesson performed by the prophet. This sign-act, like most others, follows a three-step progression.

*Command to Perform the Action (Jer. 32:6–7).* God told Jeremiah that his cousin **Hanamel** (v. 7) was going to ask him to redeem or purchase a piece of family property. According to the covenant obligations, land was to remain within the tribal inheritance. When a family member became destitute and needed to sell the property, one of the next of kin was to "redeem" the property if someone outside the family had purchased it, or to preemptively purchase the property so as to retain it within the larger family holdings.

Hanamel's property was in Jeremiah's hometown of **Anathoth** (v. 7), about three miles north of Jerusalem. The field was probably under the control of the Babylonians. Perhaps they were even encamped there or had plundered it in search of food. Thus, to purchase this piece of land at this time wasn't a particularly bright financial venture.

Although God merely informed Jeremiah of Hanamel's coming and of the offer, it seems Jeremiah was to purchase the land.

---

### WORDS FROM WESLEY

*Jeremiah 32:7*

*Anathoth*—Was a city three miles from Jerusalem, allotted out of the tribe of Benjamin for the priests. (ENOT, Jer. 1:1)

---

*Performance of the Action (Jer. 32:8–14).* Things happened just as the Lord had told Jeremiah, which to Jeremiah was a confirmation that **this was the word of the Lord** (v. 8).

Jeremiah **bought the field** (v. 9) by performing all the legal requirements necessary for the transference of ownership of property. The purchase price in **silver** was **weighed out** at **seventeen shekels** (about seven ounces of silver, vv. 9–10). Since there was no minted coin at that time, it was necessary to weigh out the appropriate amount on a balance scale. A two-part legal **deed** of purchase was drawn up that had both a **sealed copy containing the terms and conditions, as well as the unsealed copy** (v. 11). Such refers to the practice of duplicate copies of the deed on the same page. The deed was written on half of the papyrus, which was then rolled and sealed with a lump of moist clay into which was pressed the identifying inscription using an engraved stone seal, bearing in this case Jeremiah's inscription (**I signed and sealed the deed**, v. 10). When the clay hardened, it provided a permanent closure to the official document. But a copy of the deed was then written on the other half of the papyrus and left open so the terms could be examined without opening the officially sealed portion. The deed was also **witnessed**, and Jeremiah ensured the proper preservation of the document by giving it to **Baruch** (v. 13), his friend and scribe. It was customary to preserve such valuable documents in a sealed **clay jar** (v. 14), which kept out moisture and prevented deterioration.

*Interpretation (Jer. 32:15).* Once the property was transferred, Jeremiah used that real-life situation to communicate a prophetic message: **Houses, fields and vineyards will again be bought in this land** (v. 15). While the focus was on buying property, the idea is normal activities would resume in the land.

### Jeremiah's Prayer (Jer. 32:16–25)

Even though Jeremiah had faithfully obeyed, the sign-act did not seem to correlate either with the realities of the situation or with the previous prophecies of judgment Jeremiah had been consistently proclaiming. This incongruence drove Jeremiah to seek clarification from the Lord: **"Though the city will be handed over to the Babylonians, you, O Sovereign Lord, say to me, 'Buy the field'"** (v. 25).

## God's Response (Jer. 32:36–44)

As God answered Jeremiah's question, He first affirmed the truthfulness and correctness of the previous messages of Jerusalem's destruction. Yet God was also now giving a new message about what would occur *after* the judgment.

In verse 36, the NIV's sequence of **"You are saying about this city . . . but this is what the Lord . . . says"** is not to be understood as "You, Jeremiah, have mistakenly spoken of judgment on the city, whereas I am pronouncing a message of hope." Rather, the message is "You, Jeremiah, have rightly said about this city. . . . But now I, the Lord, am giving a new message that will occur after that previous word has been fulfilled."

---

### WORDS FROM WESLEY

*Jeremiah 32:8*

*They shall be my people*—By my grace I will make them holy, as the people of a holy God; and I will make them happy, as the people of the ever blessed God. (ENOT, Ezek. 37:27)

---

Verses 37–40 echo with the exuberance of God as He expressed His intent, contrasting with the judgment done in His **furious anger and great wrath** (v. 37). The message of hope is one of restoration that includes several aspects: return from the exile (v. 37); restoration to the land (vv. 37, 41); security in the land once they have been restored to it (v. 37); a renewal of the

covenant relationship (vv. 38, 40), including God's inner transforming of the people (vv. 39–40); and blessing them (vv. 39–41).

---

## WORDS FROM WESLEY

*Jeremiah 32:40*

That covenant of eternal grace
When wilt Thou make with me?
My heart I open to embrace
The God of purity:
Now let me feel Thy Spirit brought in,
And when in me Thou art,
Feel it impossible to sin,
Impossible to part.
In proof, Thou wilt not cease to love,
But still Thy servant bless,
This inbred stumbling-block remove
By perfect holiness:
I know the covenant is sure,
Seal'd with Thy Spirit's seal,
And in me, when my heart is pure,
Thou wilt for ever dwell. (PW, vol. 10, 43)

---

All of these events of restoration are spoken of as divinely
initiated and carried out. Rather than the people repenting before
God acts, here God even does the necessary inner transformation
so the people can respond properly to Him.

Verse 42 summarizes the whole divine response: yes, God
will bring **great calamity on this people**, but these are not His
final actions. He will also assuredly **give them all the prosperity**
(literally, "good") He had **promised them.**

Verses 43–44 return to the message of the sign-act, affirming
that message. But the affirmation includes an ever-widening geo-
graphical circumference: land will not only be bought in Benjamin,
but all around Jerusalem, all over Judah, all over the hill country
to the north (that is, the old nation of Israel), as well as to the

western foothills extending to the coast and to the south. The restoration to the land will be a resettlement of the whole Promised Land.

The purpose of this message is to communicate hope to God's people, even when a situation seems hopeless. When applying this message it must be kept in mind that: (1) the message is corporate, not necessarily individual, in nature; (2) it was a message of hope for the future; and (3) just because God has a hopeful future for His people does not exclude God's disciplining and punishing His people for their sin in the present. However, such punishment is never God's final objective. God's ultimate intent is restoration and renewal of the relationship with Him.

## DISCUSSION

Tell about a time when a hope or dream you had for your life was fulfilled.

1. Redemption is a constant theme in this story. Describe what it means to you to redeem someone or something.

2. What other Bible stories tell of people who were filled with faith in spite of their circumstances?

3. Jeremiah was both encouraging and truthful. Do you think it is always possible to be both?

4. Why do you think God allows faithful people to suffer?

5. Compare and contrast God's sense of timing with the nine months of pregnancy.

6. Why is it unwise to get ahead of (or behind) God's timeline in your life?

7. Jeremiah bought a piece of land as an act of hope. What practical action could you take to show that you trust God for the future?

8. If the "fear of the LORD" is really a deep sense of respect for God, how would you rate your attitude toward God?

9. What thoughts or actions help you to gain a sense of peace when life doesn't seem to make sense?

## PRAYER

Father, we offer You our old, worthless life in exchange for a new and abundant one.

# 5

# EXPERIENCING GOD'S DISCIPLINE

*Lamentations 3:19–40*

We grow through God's discipline.

When a child is disciplined by his or her parents, is that a good thing or a bad thing? While none of us likes the idea of facing a time-out or a swat on the bottom, adults at least would recognize that discipline, though painful, is a good thing. We correct our children because we love them and want better things for them in the future.

God does the same for us. We see that Jeremiah, the weeping prophet, is nothing short of heartsick over the ruin of his beloved Jerusalem. Yet amid this devastation, he sees God's hand at work. This study looks at the positive side of God's discipline and will enable you to find hope for your future in spite of the difficulties you may now be facing.

## COMMENTARY

Tradition tells us that Jeremiah wrote this book soon after the fall of Jerusalem, after the Babylonians took the people of Judah into exile (586 B.C.). The theme of grief fits Jeremiah's depressive personality well; the word *lament* appears occasionally in Jeremiah (see 7:29; 9:10, 20). Jeremiah realized how Judah deserved its punishment, but that did little to relieve the grief he felt.

Five songs comprise Lamentations. Fortunately, they reveal a progression from despair toward hope. Broadly speaking, the songs (one per chapter) include the following themes: (1) the pain Jeremiah and his countrymen had experienced (see 1:1–2);

(2) that pain as God's punishment for Judah's sin (2:1–2); (3) the turning point—God through Jeremiah offers the possibility of comfort and restoration (3:22–26); (4) further exploration of sin and restoration (4:13, 22); and (5) God's people crying out for His mercy (5:19–22).

Jeremiah took great care in writing this book. In contrast to the longer recorded prophecy of Jeremiah, Lamentations is laid out in a most structured manner. Note the following repeated patterns:

|  | Chapter 1 | Chapter 2 | Chapter 3 | Chapter 4 | Chapter 5 |
|---|---|---|---|---|---|
| Number of verses | 22 | 22 | 66 (22 tripled) | 22 | 22 |
| Acrostic?* | Yes | Yes | Yes# | Yes | No |
| Lines per verse | 3 (except 1:7) | 3 | 1 | 2 | 1 |
| Total lines per chapter | 66 | 66 | 66 | 44 | 22 |

*The word *acrostic* designates a literary pattern where the first word in each verse (in the original Hebrew) begins with a successive letter of the Hebrew alphabet.

#In chapter 3, not only does the first word in each verse begin with the appropriate letter, the first word in all three lines of each verse (in the original Hebrew) also begin with that letter.

## The Strength of Jeremiah's Grief (Lam. 3:19–20)

Jeremiah never sugarcoated the pain God's people were experiencing. Even in this Scripture passage, perhaps the brightest point in the entire book, Jeremiah still placed the light of hope in the context of the surrounding darkness.

**"I remember my affliction and my wandering"** (v. 19). **Affliction** refers to the pain of being forced away from home. **Wandering** connotes the search for a new place to settle. **Bitterness:** Jeremiah compared the entire experience to a bitter taste on his mouth. In the Old Testament, **gall** usually referred to a poisonous herb (see Deut.

29:18, where the same Hebrew word is translated "bitter poison"). Two verses later, Jeremiah would turn to face the light, but in these verses we sense the oppressive darkness.

## The Strength of Jeremiah's Hope (Lam. 3:21–24)

As Jeremiah wrote the two preceding verses, he remembered the pain God's people had known. Fortunately, that was not all he remembered. He could also **call to mind** (v. 21) the character of his God and the promises He had made. From his earliest days, Jeremiah had heard how God had chosen the descendants of Abraham as His people. God had instructed His people to follow Him. God had promised blessings for obedience and punishment for disobedience. The people had disobeyed, and God had sent the promised punishment. Even so, God had promised to restore those who repented. Jeremiah knew God had never turned His back on His people. He had allowed exile to come, not to destroy them but to show them the urgency of returning to and maintaining a strong relationship with Him. "My circumstances look bleak," Jeremiah thought, "but my God has not changed. **Therefore I have hope**."

If God had given up on His people, He might have destroyed them (see v. 22). Once, back in the earliest days of the human race, God wiped out nearly all life (Gen. 6–8). Centuries later, after His people's idolatry at the base of Mount Sinai, He nearly destroyed the descendants of Abraham. Since that time, God had threatened punishment by exile for His people (beginning in Deut. 28:63–68). In Jeremiah's lifetime, God had carried through on that promise. But God's character had not changed. He remained "the compassionate and gracious God, slow to anger, abounding in love and faithfulness" (Ex. 34:6). Perhaps Jeremiah considered those very words from the mouth of God as he continued his song: **His compassions never fail . . . great** (in size beyond any scope of measurement) **is your faithfulness** (vv. 22–23). If God's love for His people was infinite, then He would rescue them from their exile, even if they deserved that trial.

---

### WORDS FROM WESLEY

*Lamentations 3:23*

*Faithfulness*—In fulfilling thy promises to thy people. (ENOT)

---

**"The LORD is my portion"** (v. 24). By analogy, those words demonstrate Jeremiah's complete dependence on God. They likely allude to the division of Canaan as the Israelites were about to enter the Promised Land. All the tribes of Israel were allotted land, except the priests and the Levites. For their living, they were not to depend on farming; they were to depend on God (see Num. 18:20–24). God himself took the place of their land allotment; He was their portion. Jeremiah, at this point, could not live on land he owned. On whom did he depend? On God himself.

**"Therefore I will wait for him"** (v. 24). In this context, waiting is much more than enduring the passage of time, impatiently questioning the cause of delay. Waiting here involves eager anticipation of God's yet unseen deliverance (see Isa. 40:31).

### The Strength of Jeremiah's Patience (Lam. 3:25–30)

At this point, Jeremiah chose to move from the first person (I) to the third person (those, him). Within these verses, Jeremiah gave further attention to all those who patiently wait for God to act.

Note in the first three verses the repetition of the word *good*. Three verses yield three different "goods." God is **good**. Therefore it is **good** to wait for Him. It's **good** for those waiting to be **young**. The first two ideas make sense easily; they require little explanation. But the third? Waiting, even in eager expectation is nonetheless waiting. If the people had recently gone into exile, it would be seventy years before God would bring them home again. God continued to love His people. He had not forgotten them. He would restore them to their homeland, but not until long after Jeremiah and his generation had died.

Did Jeremiah know how long the exile would be? Perhaps. Did Jeremiah know he would die in exile? Probably. Yet he still trusted God. (Compare Jeremiah with those the writer of Heb. 11 includes in his "hall of faith," those who were "commended for their faith, [even though] none of them received what had been promised" [11:39].).

Young people might be waiting for a while; what should they do in the meantime? Endure. God is good. God will restore Judah. But here Jeremiah again dropped hints that in the meantime, the young people might face more affliction, wandering, bitterness, and gall (Lam. 3:19).

---

## WORDS FROM WESLEY

*Lamentations 3:27*

*Bear*—quietly and patiently to bear what afflictions God will please to lay upon us. And if God tame us when *young*, by his word or by his rod, it is an unspeakable advantage. (ENOT)

---

They should **sit** waiting **. . . in silence** (v. 28). Do those words imply that they should not speak any words of grief or anger? If so, then Jeremiah broke those very instructions even before finishing this song (3:42–51). God prefers honesty to deception, even when His people are feeling upset. His people could take their grief to God, but He might turn around and remind them of the sin that took them into exile—**for the LORD has laid it** (the yoke of suffering) **on him** (a young person waiting, v. 28).

While waiting, the young person should **bury his face in the dust** (v. 29). Picture the ancients grieving in sackcloth and ashes (compare Job 16:15). "Grief, yes," Jeremiah wrote, "But even as the pain continues, don't give up **hope**" (Lam. 3:29).

The next picture of the ongoing stress (a **strike** on the **cheek**, v. 30) again reflects the experience of Job (16:10) and also fore-shadows Jesus, who willingly entered the exile of death (Matt. 27:30). Job, and subsequently Jesus, experienced public **disgrace** (Lam. 3:30), and they both came out of the darkness into the light. God's people would likewise continue in shame, but ultimately find restoration.

### The Strength of Jeremiah's Faith (Lam. 3:31–39)

That shame for a period with restoration following, is precisely the content of verse 31: God's people **are not cast off forever**.

The next two verses offer first a surprisingly strong sentence but then two qualifying statements. The surprise? God **brings grief** (v. 32). Sometimes we blame God for problems we face, but then catch ourselves with the thought, "God gives only good gifts." Can God give *bad* gifts that produce grief? No, but He does give good gifts that His followers do not easily recognize as good. God's primary concern for His children is not their happiness but their growth. What kind of God would give nothing but goodies to a nation (Judah) that had turned its back on Him? God wished His people to follow Him. He offered blessings as motivation to obey, but punishment for disobedience. God keeps His promises, but that's not the only reason God gave grief to His people. He hoped that appearing to abandon them would show them how much they needed Him, and thus bring them back to himself.

The qualifiers? First, though He may cause His children pain, He cannot bear to leave them in punishment forever. His unfailing love brings His compassion once again. The exile would end; the people would return home.

Second, **he does not willingly bring affliction** (v. 33). God would prefer that His children follow Him so He could continually shower His blessings on them. Just as no parent wishes to punish his or her child, God wishes He could avoid causing people pain. God has to change His first plan to do what will be best for those He loves.

---

### WORDS FROM WESLEY

*Lamentations 3:33*

*Willingly*—Not from His own mere motion without a cause given Him from the persons afflicted. Hence judgment is called God's strange work. (ENOT)

---

While His people wait, while they endure even decades in exile, they need not fear that the God of **unfailing love** (v. 32) has actually turned His back on them. It might have appeared God did not see, but Jeremiah stated in faith that nothing escaped God's notice. Jeremiah listed examples of events that God had carefully observed: the Babylonians crushing **underfoot** (v. 34) God's people—the aggressors in time would get back what they had given out (see Hab. 2:16–17). But prior to the exile God had also observed Judah's sins, for example, people's attempts to **deprive** others of their **rights** to God and **justice** (Lam. 3:35–36). God had seen Judah's sin and had taken appropriate action to show His people the seriousness of their actions.

Verses 37–39 again offer a trilogy of thoughts. God is the only one in true control. God alone can **speak** (v. 37), knowing without doubt that His word will change the world. When God speaks, both **calamities and good things come** (v. 38). In all things God engineers, He intends to show His love. Sometimes that is obvious to us. Other times, His love appears to be harsh and unfair. When

God sends calamity as punishment for a person's sin, that person should have known it was coming. God may have allowed the pain, but the person's free choice of sin led God to His severe action. The sinner has no one to blame but him- or herself. (We must, of course, avoid the common fallacy that all suffering is the result of sin. God inspired an entire biblical book—Job—to counter that misunderstanding.)

---

### WORDS FROM WESLEY

*Lamentations 3:37*

*Who*—Nothing comes to pass in the world, but by the disposal of divine providence. This seems to be spoken in the name of the people of God, arguing themselves into a quiet submission, to their afflictions, from the consideration of the hand of God in them. (ENOT)

---

## Jeremiah's Call to the People to Imitate Him (Lam. 3:40)

After all that, Jeremiah closed this passage with a simple request: Each of us as individuals, all of us collectively as a nation, needs to **examine** him- or herself (v. 40). Ongoing sin merely leads to ongoing pain. The pain of exile is already bad enough; if only we return to God, then we could more easily sense His great love and faithfulness.

## DISCUSSION

Describe the relationship between faith and hope.

1. Jeremiah wrote these words after Jerusalem had been besieged and destroyed. From his words, describe the circumstances he faced.

2. How would you describe Jeremiah's mood in this passage — pessimistic or optimistic? Why?

3. What can you discern from these verses about the character of God?

4. Jeremiah faced the loss of his city and nation. What kinds of losses are we likely to face?

5. Is it wrong for a Christian to feel discouraged? Why or why not?

6. Jeremiah said God's compassion is renewed every day. In what ways have you experienced God's grace in spite of difficult circumstances?

7. If God gave you a toolbox for coping with loss, what would be in it?

8. Which of these spiritual tools has proved to be the most comforting to you?

## PRAYER

Lord, help us not to shy away from Your correction; it is one of many signs You love us.

# 6

# WHEN GOD SPEAKS

*Ezekiel 1:1, 25–28; 2:1–8*

---

When God speaks, we must listen and obey.

If God were to speak to you, how would you know you were hearing His voice? If you were certain God had spoken to you, what would you do? Throughout history, God has spoken individually to a number of people, some of them seemingly unlikely candidates. Moses, Gideon, Samuel, and Isaiah all had trouble believing God would single them out for a task—or that they were worthy of such a calling.

Like those heroes of old, Ezekiel was called by God. The record of his commissioning holds important lessons for all of us, for any one of us might be called as well. This study will help you recognize the voice of God and motivate you to listen closely and obey.

## COMMENTARY

Ezekiel had been taken into exile to Babylonia along with others of the upper classes of Judah in 597 B.C., some ten years before Jerusalem's destruction. The Babylonian policy of deporting massive groups of people from conquered territories was to resettle them in largely unpopulated areas of Babylonia so as to rebuild those areas. The group of which Ezekiel was a part was resettled in Tel Abib, probably an older abandoned or destroyed city along the Kebar River.

### Ezekiel Received a Vision from God (Ezek. 1:1)

While in exile, Ezekiel received a vision from God (**"I saw visions of God,"** v. 1). The plural, **visions**, is probably a plural of intensification that indicates the divine source rather than the specific content. This vision (1:1—3:15) is the account of the call of Ezekiel to prophetic ministry.

This vision occurred in **the thirtieth year, in the fourth month on the fifth day** (v. 1), which is correlated in verse 2 to "the fifth year of the exile of King Jehoiachin," thus 593 B.C. There is uncertainty as to what occasion **the thirtieth year** refers. Among the best suggestions is that it refers to the thirtieth year of Ezekiel's life, although this is not the typical way in Hebrew to indicate a person's age. The significance of Ezekiel being thirty years old lies in the fact that he was a priest. When someone of priestly descent turned thirty, he embarked on active ministry in the temple. But because Ezekiel was in exile, physical separation from the temple prevented him from performing such a ministry. Thus at the point he would have entered into priestly ministry in the temple, God called him to a different type of ministry, that of being a prophet.

---

### WORDS FROM WESLEY

*Ezekiel 1:1*

*Thirtieth year*—From the finding the book of the law in the eighteenth year of Josiah, from which date to the fifth year of the captivity are thirty years. *Fifth day*—Probably it was the sabbath day, when the Jews were at leisure to hear the prophet. *River*—Perhaps retiring thither to lament their own sins, and Jerusalem's desolation. *Chebar*—A river now called Giulap, arising out of the mountain Masius, and falling into Euphrates, somewhat below a city called by the same name. (ENOT)

## Divine Revelation (Ezek. 1:25–28)

The first part of the vision was the revelation of God himself to Ezekiel. The vision initially involved a storm consisting of a cloud with lightning and brilliant light (1:4), elements common to a theophany—a personal revelation of God.

As the cloud approached, Ezekiel began to distinguish specific features within the cloud. He first saw four living creatures (vv. 5–14), composed of both human and animal forms. These creatures, which he later identified as cherubim (10:1–17), are often spoken of as being part of the heavenly entourage in the divine presence (see 1 Kings 6:23–28; 1 Sam. 4:4; Ps. 80:1; 99:1). Here they are also representative of animated life. Thus the four faces symbolize the four earthly "animal" domains: man equals humans; lion equals wild beasts; ox equals domesticated beasts; eagle equals birds. Associated with the "living creatures" is that they are bearing a wheeled vehicle that moves as they move (Ezek. 1:15–21).

In verses 25–28, the focus shifts to that which is on the platform or floor (the expanse) of the chariot. The description has progressively moved from the lower parts of the vision objects to the upper elements. The impression is that out of reverence and awe Ezekiel has lowered his eyes, and only gradually is raising them to focus on the ultimate content of the vision, that which is **above the expanse** (v. 25).

It is just prior to this description in verses 25–28 that the auditory elements have been introduced into the account. Just like the visual elements of the cloud and lightning (fire, brightness) are common to theophanies, so too is this description of the "sound" as God speaks (see Ex. 19:9). This emphasis (Ezek. 1:25, 28) on the **voice** is central to the call narrative of a prophet, because Ezekiel was being called to be the "voice" of God among the people.

Besides the element of the voice, Ezekiel described two other elements above the expanse. The first is that of **a throne**, and the second is that of **a figure like that of a man** (v. 26) who was seated on that throne. Obviously the throne indicates that the one on it is a "kingly" figure. And because of the previous description of the creatures and expanse that indicate the elements of creation, the "figure" is clearly the acknowledged king over all of creation.

Ezekiel hesitated to name any of the elements of the visions by actually saying they "are" something. Rather he described them as being "like" something. So, that which is above the expanse is **what looked like a throne**, and the **figure** was **like that of a man** (v. 26). In describing the figure, note the deference: **from what appeared to be his waist up he looked like glowing metal . . . he looked like fire** (v. 27). The revelation of God can only be described in comparisons, without actually declaring this is the very substance of God.

---

### WORDS FROM WESLEY

*Ezekiel 1:27*

*Amber*—In this colour does Christ appear against the rebellious Jews; He that would have visited them clothed with the garments of salvation, now puts on the garments of vengeance, expressed by such metaphors. *Brightness*—Majesty, justice, and unstained holiness, shine round about Him. (ENOT)

---

The first descriptions of the throne-chariot emphasize its brilliant quality. Similar are the descriptions in verses 25–28: the throne is of something like **sapphire** (v. 25); the upper portion of the figure **looked like glowing metal, as if full of fire,** while the lower portion **looked like fire; and brilliant light surrounded him** (vv. 25–26); and the summarizing conclusion of the whole is that it is **like the appearance of a rainbow in the clouds on a rainy day, so was the radiance around him** (v. 28). Even the description attempts to overawe with its brightness and spectacular color.

Finally, Ezekiel identified the "figure": **This was the appearance of the likeness of the glory of the Lord** (v. 28). Ezekiel recognized that he had seen a vision of the very glory of the Lord. The only fitting response was for him to fall **facedown** in an act of worshipful reverence and submission.

Although the revelation of the glory of God is magnificent, God did not appear to Ezekiel for the purpose of merely revealing His majesty and grandeur, but rather for the purpose of calling Ezekiel to be His spokesperson. Most "call visions" have this element because it must be firmly fixed in the potential prophet's mind whom he is to represent and speak for.

Amid the revelation of himself, God fully took the initiative to call the prophet. The vision was unsolicited and broke into Ezekiel's normal routine. Thus God also took the initiative in speaking: **I heard the voice of one speaking** (v. 28).

### Introductory Divine Word (Ezek. 2:1–2)

Five times in three verses (1:28 — 2:2) there is emphasis on God speaking: "I heard the voice of one speaking" (1:28), **He said to me** (2:1), **"I will speak to you"** (v. 1), **As he spoke** (v. 2), and **I heard him speaking to me** (v. 2). Since Ezekiel was being called to be a messenger for God, he needed to be able to discern and hear the voice of God if he was to faithfully transmit the messages.

---

### WORDS FROM WESLEY
#### Ezekiel 2:1

*And* — He that sat upon the throne, Jesus Christ. *Son of man* — A phrase which is ninety-five times at least used in this prophecy to keep him humble who had such great revelations. *Stand* — Arise, fear not. And with this command God sent forth a power enabling him to rise and stand. (ENOT)

Whereas the previous bowing with one's face down indicates submission, standing in the presence of the King indicates a posture of listening with a willingness and readiness to then immediately leave the royal presence to carry out what the King has commissioned (see Neh. 8:5).

In this case, it seems the revelation had so overwhelmed Ezekiel that he was incapable of standing, even though commanded to do so (**stand up on your feet**, Ezek. 2:1). As God spoke, He also empowered Ezekiel through the **Spirit** (v. 2). This empowering to "hear" the divine word is indicative of the whole prophetic ministry—it comes through God, not through the individual being called.

The humanness of Ezekiel is also stressed through the title by which God addressed Ezekiel: **son of man** (vv. 1, 3, 8). The term is akin to saying "human," and underscores the distinction between God, who has just appeared in a "figure like that of a man," and Ezekiel. (The use of the term in Ezekiel must be clearly distinguished from its use in the vision of Dan. 7 and as a common title for Jesus, where divinity rather than humanity is being stressed.)

## Commissioning (Ezek. 2:3–5)

Ezekiel was being sent out from the presence of God to transmit God's messages to the people. The command and terse summary of the message is: **Say to them, "This is what the Sovereign Lord says"** (v. 4). Ezekiel was to be the mouthpiece for God proclaiming *only* what God tells him to. The messenger is not the originator of the message, merely the transmitter of it.

God identified Ezekiel's audience: **the Israelites** (v. 3). But the commissioning also carried an extensive and unflattering description of these people: **a rebellious nation that has rebelled against me** (v. 3); they **are obstinate and stubborn** (v. 4); and again, **they are a rebellious house** (v. 5).

---

## WORDS FROM WESLEY

### Ezekiel 2:5

*Shall know*—They that obey shall know by the good I will do them, those that will not, by the evil which I will bring upon them. (ENOT)

---

## Reassurance and the Difficulty of the Task (Ezek. 2:6–8)

This stress on the rebelliousness of the people has direct implications for Ezekiel's prophetic ministry: Since the people were against God, they would also be against Ezekiel. He was not speaking to an audience who would readily receive the messages he would be proclaiming for God. In fact, the situation Ezekiel found himself in would be akin to dealing with **briers and thorns** and **scorpions** (v. 6). In other words, the very real danger and potential existed for Ezekiel to be severely wounded. The prophetic task and ministry would not be an easy job. We must divorce ourselves from the concept that a call by God to ministry means a life of ease and "success" in the sense of people readily responding to the Word of God and flocking into our churches. In some contexts this may occur, but in many other contexts there will be a lack of response, resistance, and even physical persecution. Such also characterized Jesus' ministry (see John 1:10–11), and He told His followers to accept it as well (see Luke 21:12; John 15:18–21).

In light of the people's rebelliousness and lack of receptivity, God reassured Ezekiel that he should **not be afraid** to carry out the prophetic task (three times in v. 6). In 3:9, God told him He would empower Ezekiel and make him capable to withstand the people's opposition.

As God called Ezekiel, He also stressed that the issue for Ezekiel was not whether the people would respond, but rather his faithfulness in carrying out the prophetic ministry (**"You**

**must speak my words to them, whether they listen or fail to listen,"** v. 7). Ezekiel's "success" would not be measured by the number of "converts" he had, but by whether he had faithfully proclaimed God's messages.

What is of utmost importance is that the divine word had been proclaimed, so that when the judgment actually came upon the people for their sins, they had no excuse. The prophet delivered the messages that forewarned the people. They would be unable to say to God, "We didn't know You considered what we were doing was sin" or "We didn't know You were about to punish us for what we have been doing."

The other element God stressed to Ezekiel was that Ezekiel was to model a response to God that directly contrasted the rebelliousness of the people: **"But you, son of man . . . do not rebel like that rebellious house"** (v. 8). Whereas the people were disobedient in adhering faithfully to God's word, Ezekiel was to model complete obedience. The Hebrew phrase **listen** means more than just hearing. It involves acting on what was heard.

A demonstration of Ezekiel's obedience was immediately called for. God told him to **"eat what I give you"** (v. 8). In the following verses, Ezekiel saw a scroll he was commanded to eat. In obedience, he did. The implication of this for his prophetic ministry was that he had to ingest the divine word before he could proclaim it to the people. Similarly, the divine word must be part of our lives before we can credibly proclaim it to others.

## DISCUSSION

List some symptoms of spiritual deafness. Tell about the last time you experienced this.

1. Describe the appearance of the being Ezekiel saw. What spiritual qualities do you think those physical characteristics represent?

2. Ezekiel's posture showed reverence. When the Holy Spirit helped him stand, what did that signify?

3. Why did God send Ezekiel to preach? Why would God do this if He knew the preaching would not be effective?

4. Has there ever been a time when you were unresponsive to God? Explain.

5. Tell about a time that you felt God speaking to you and you listened.

6. What habits or practices make us better able to hear the voice of God?

7. What habits or practices make us more disposed to obey God?

8. What do you believe your response would be when you met God face-to-face?

## PRAYER

Father, help us to know and do Your will.

# REPENT AND LIVE!

*Ezekiel 18:20–32*

God offers the opportunity to repent and live.

How do you deal with your own failures? Some choose denial, believing they have not done wrong or are at least no worse than anyone else. Some respond by blaming their upbringing, their genetics, their circumstances, or other people. Still others address their moral shortcomings by trying to balance the scale, adding more and more good behaviors to counterbalance the bad.

This study points to the one effective way to deal with sin—repentance. Only through confession and repentance will we find forgiveness and new life.

## COMMENTARY

There is a *Peanuts* cartoon in which Lucy says, "I want to talk to you, Charlie Brown. As your sister's consulting psychiatrist, I must put the blame for her fears on you!" Charlie responds, "On *me*?" To which Lucy replies, "Each generation must be able to blame the previous generation for its problems. It doesn't solve anything, but it makes us all feel better!" The prophecy of Ezekiel 18 was motivated by a similar attitude, summarized in the proverb of verse 2: "The fathers eat sour grapes and the children's teeth are set on edge." The people were seeking to avoid responsibility by asserting that they were suffering for the sins of the previous generation.

This prophecy is a "disputation" speech, which means that the position of the people is being refuted through the subsequent prophetic word. The prophecy moves through three sections, each serving a different, yet interrelated, persuasive function: (1) to counter the people's position (vv. 4–20); (2) to lay out a theology of repentance (vv. 21–29); and (3) to call the people to repent.

### Individual Responsibility before God (Ezek. 18:20)

**The soul who sins is the one who will die** (v. 20). Verse 20 concludes the first section and reiterates the principle that each individual (generation) is held accountable and receives the punishment for his or her personal sins. The Hebrew term translated by the NIV as **soul** is not just the spiritual part of the person. Rather, the term refers to persons as living beings. **Will die** in this passage refers to physical, rather than spiritual, death.

That general principle is then made more specific: **The son will not share the guilt of the father, nor will the father share the guilt of the son.** The term **guilt** in the Hebrew is *iniquity*, which in Hebrew can mean both the sinful deed as well as the consequences. In this instance, it means having been found legally guilty for the crime and thus under sentence of punishment.

This section (vv. 4–20) is meant to convince the people that their suffering is a result of their own sin, not that of the previous generation.

### Theology of Repentance (Ezek. 18:21–29)

As long as the people blamed others for their predicament, they would never correct the situation. But if they could accept responsibility for their suffering, their response would alter the judgment. This is the goal of verses 21–29.

Just as accountability for sins does not transfer from one generation to the next, so it can be that a person's accountability for their own sins does not transfer from the past to the present.

This concept is illustrated through two separate cases that are repeated in a mirroring pattern. The cases are developed around a fivefold pattern. The only deviation from the pattern is that in the second occurrence of the two cases (vv. 27–28 and v. 26), the fourth element is lacking.

1. The person (wicked or righteous) "turns away from" his or her current behavior:

| Case 1: Verses 21–22 and 27–28 | Case 2: Verses 24 and 26 |
| --- | --- |
| 21 But if a wicked man turns away from all the sins he has committed | 24 But if a righteous man turns from his righteousness |
| 27 But if a wicked man turns away from the wickedness he has committed | 26 If a righteous man turns from his righteousness |

2. The person does the opposite of his or her previous behavior:

| | |
| --- | --- |
| 21 and keeps all my decrees and does what is just and right, | 24 and commits sin and does the same detestable things the wicked man does, |
| 27 and does what is just and right, | 26 and commits sin, |

3. The sentence, based on the newly adopted behavior, is declared:

| | |
| --- | --- |
| 21 he will surely live, he will not die. | 24 will he live? |
| 27 he will save his life. | 26 he will die for it; |

4. A statement that the actions from which he or she turned away will not be remembered against him or her is given:

| | |
| --- | --- |
| 22 None of the offenses he has committed will be remembered against him. | 24 None of the righteous things he has done will be remembered. |

5. The verdict and sentence are restated:

| 22 Because of the righteous things he has done, he will live. | 24 Because of the unfaithfulness he is guilty of and because of the sins he has committed, he will die. |
|---|---|
| 28 Because he considers all the offenses he has committed and turns away from them, he will surely live; he will not die. | 26 because of the sin he has committed he will die. |

## The Wicked Who Repent (Ezek. 18:21–22, 27–28)

In the first element of case 1 (also v. 23), **turns** (v. 21) is the Hebrew for *repents* and involves two aspects: turning away from wickedness, and turning toward God. Repentance is not merely adding God onto our current lives without making any alterations, but rather it is abandoning the sinful practices and behaviors that are contrary to God's holiness.

The point of case 1 is to show the effectiveness of repentance: *If* the wicked person repents, *then* the sentence of death is replaced with the declaration of life. This change is reinforced by the declaration that the previous offenses will no longer be **remembered against him** (v. 22). In Hebrew, the concept of remember is not primarily the mental capability to recall a past event, but rather that the person is held accountable for past behaviors and that the current relationship is based on the person's past behavior. Thus "not to remember" something against a person is to treat him or her as if the past never occurred.

## God's Desire (Ezek. 18:23)

The principle of this verse is expressed through a two-part rhetorical question: **"Do I take any pleasure in the death of the wicked?"** The implied answer is clearly a negative. So even though death is the pronounced judgment against the wicked, the repetition of that sentence does not imply that this is something

God desires. And because He does not take pleasure in it, there is an alternative, which is expressed in the second rhetorical question: **"Rather, am I not pleased when they turn from their ways and live?"** The unexpressed answer is, of course, yes. God's delight is in the righteous person upon whom He pronounces "he will surely live" (vv. 9, 17, 19).

---

### WORDS FROM WESLEY

*Ezekiel 18:23*

O that God would give me the desire of my heart! That He would grant the thing which I long for! Even that your mind might now be free and calm, and open to the light of his Spirit! That you would impartially consider how it is possible to reconcile reprobation with the following Scriptures . . . "The soul that sinneth, it shall die. The son shall not bear" (eternally) "the iniquity of the father, neither shall the father bear the iniquity of the son. Have I any pleasure at all that the wicked should die? saith the Lord; and not that he should return from his ways, and live?" (Ezek. 18:20, 23). (WJW. vol. 10, 211–212)

---

## The Righteous Who Turn to Wickedness (Ezek. 18:24, 26)

The two cases given here illustrate a broader concept than just repentance: that God evaluates a person on the individual's current relationship with Him, not on past experience. Such is true for the wicked that if they turn and repent, a new pronouncement of "life" is given (case 1).

In the case of the righteous person, the same overarching principle applies: God evaluates people on their current relationship with Him, not on their past. God is not primarily concerned about our being able to point to some event in the past where we "accepted Christ," but rather evaluates us on our current walk with Him.

---

## WORDS FROM WESLEY

### Ezekiel 18:24

On this authority, I believe a saint may fall away; that one who is holy or righteous in the judgment of God himself may nevertheless so fall from God as to perish everlastingly.

For thus saith the Lord: "When the righteous turneth away from his righteousness, and committeth iniquity; in his trespass that he hath trespassed, and in his sin that he hath sinned, in them shall he die" (Ezek. 18:24).

That this is to be understood of eternal death appears from the twenty-sixth verse: "When a righteous man turneth away from his righteousness and committeth iniquity, and dieth in them" (here is temporal death); "for his iniquity that he hath done he shall die." (Here is death eternal.) (WJW, vol. 10, 285)

---

## The People's Response (Ezek. 18:25, 29)

The people respond: **"The way of the Lord is not just"** (v. 25). But why would they not accept this teaching? Repentance offers hope! The other issue is what **way of the Lord** are they critiquing — His acts of judgment or the principles by which He functions?

Two possible solutions seem to fit the context. The first is to understand the people's objection as a protest in the sense that they still maintain their innocence. Thus, if God *only* passes judgment on the wicked, then they, though innocent, are experiencing judgment, which means God is not dealing with them justly.

The other possibility is that the people believed that sin must be equally balanced by punishment and that one should be evaluated by one's whole life. If a person was very wicked for all her life but had a "deathbed conversion" experience, certainly she should be evaluated by her whole life, not just the last few moments of it. By granting forgiveness, God is allowing the previous wickedness to go unpunished and therefore the wickedness and punishment are not balancing out. Likewise, if one walked with

God for the majority of one's life, surely that should outweigh a recent lapse into sin. Thus, according to the people's way of thinking, God's sentence of death on the righteous person who has turned to wickedness is not balancing out all of the previous righteousness, and is thus unjust. If this is the point of the criticism, then the people may be acknowledging that they had sinned a little, but surely their previous righteousness should outweigh any current minor indiscretions.

God emphatically counters their assertion through two rhetorical questions: **"Is my way unjust?"** Of course not! **"Is it not your ways that are unjust?"** (v. 29). Here the implied answer is yes. In other words, the way in which God is dealing with His people is fully in accordance with the covenant obligations and stipulations.

---

### WORDS FROM WESLEY
#### *Ezekiel 18:31*

"Why will you die, O house of Israel?" (Ezek. 18:31). God warns you of the approaching judgment, that ye may take warning, and escape it by timely repentance. He lifts up His hand, and shakes it over you, that ye may see it, and prevent the stroke. He tells you, "Now is the axe laid unto the root of the trees" (Matt. 3:10). Therefore repent; bring forth good fruit; and ye shall not be hewn down, and cast into the fire. O do not despise the riches of His mercy, but let it lead you to repentance! "Account that the longsuffering of the Lord is salvation" (2 Pet. 3:15). Harden not your hearts, but turn to Him that smites you; or, rather, threatens to smite, that ye may turn and be spared!

How slow is the Lord to anger! How unwilling to punish! By what leisurely steps does He come to take vengeance! How many lighter afflictions before the final blow! (WJW, vol. 7. 397)

---

### Call to Repent (Ezek. 18:30–32)

The climax to which the previous arguments have been moving is the call to repentance: Since they *are* being held responsible for their own sins, and since repentance *can* alter their status with God, they should turn back to God. The call to repent is stated twice, and both statements contain three parts: (1) a restatement of the principle; (2) a call to repent in the grammatical imperative; and (3) personal motivation for repentance.

| | **Verses 30–31** | **Verse 32** |
|---|---|---|
| Restatement of Principle | 30 I will judge you, each one according to his ways (vv. 4–20). | 32 I take no pleasure in the death of anyone (vv. 21–29). |
| Call to Repent | 30 Repent! Turn away from all your offenses. 31 Rid yourselves of all the offenses you have committed, and get a new heart and a new spirit. | 32 Repent |
| Motivation | 30 then sin will not be your downfall. 31 Why will you die, O house of Israel? | 32 and live! |

Repentance is not only a turning away from wickedness, but also a turning toward God, here expressed as **get a new heart and a new spirit** (v. 31).

The call to repentance is addressed to the people and thus focuses on the human element in the process rather than the divine. The inner transformational work involves not only the divine element, but also the human desire and will. Without the human response or repentance, God cannot perform the inner work of transformation He longs to accomplish; and without the divine work, humans remain unable to generate the necessary inner change.

## DISCUSSION

Explain the difference between inner conversion and outer conversion.

1. What is the relationship between our actions, the condition of our heart, and our standing before God, according to Ezekiel?

2. Ezekiel raised the question of whether God takes pleasure in the spiritual death of any person. Why might some people think God would delight in punishing? Do you think He does? Explain.

3. God alone can make a new heart, yet He expected people to play some part in their transformation. What was it?

4. Do you think it is possible to live free from sin? Why or why not?

5. If you met someone who felt helpless to change, how would you offer hope?

6. What might cause a person to turn down God's offer of mercy?

7. When are the words "I'm sorry" insufficient to restore a relationship?

8. Do you think Christians need to repent? Why or why not?

## PRAYER

Search us, O God. See if there is any offensive way in us and lead us in your truth (see Ps. 139:23–24).

# EXPERIENCING GOD'S COMPASSION

*Ezekiel 34:7–16; Jeremiah 23:1–6*

God cares for His people.

Leaders have a unique and important role in any community, including the church. Leaders are given great authority, great influence, and have the ability to do great good—or great harm. When God's leaders perform poorly or, worse yet, become corrupt, the people suffer. Not only is the "flock" hurt, but those who watch the church from a distance as well. The headlines regularly offer examples of the damage done by such individuals.

Fortunately, God's work is greater than any one man or woman. It is not human leaders but God himself who shepherds and guides His people. This study will help us look beyond our human leaders, no matter how good they may be, to depend on God for our direction and security.

## COMMENTARY

The opening verse of Psalm 23, "The Lord is my shepherd, I shall not be in want," is one of the best-known verses in the entire Bible. The picture of a shepherd meticulously caring for his flock is one most people can understand even if they have little direct experience with sheep. These passages from Ezekiel and Jeremiah continue and expand on this description of God as a shepherd.

The settings for the messages of Jeremiah and Ezekiel are quite different. Jeremiah spent almost all his ministry in the land of Judah. He began during the reign of the last good king, Josiah

(640–609 B.C.) and lived through the succession of four weak kings over a period of about twenty-three years. He was present when the Babylonians broke through the walls of Jerusalem and captured the city (586 B.C.). The Babylonians treated him with respect and allowed him to stay in Judah (Jer. 39:11 — 40:6). Eventually he was forced to accompany rebels to Egypt (43:6–7).

While Jeremiah was present for the last days of Judah, the younger Ezekiel was already in exile. When King Nebuchadnezzar of Babylon first asserted authority over Judah, he took the first wave of exiles, which included Daniel and his three friends (605 B.C.). Later Judah rebelled against Babylon, and Nebuchadnezzar took a second wave of exiles in 597 B.C. This group included the young priest Ezekiel (Ezek. 1:1–3). This means Ezekiel was already living in Babylon when he began his ministry. He is not an eyewitness to the last days of Judah as was the older Jeremiah.

### To Shepherds Who Are Not Shepherds (Ezek. 34:7–10)

Ezekiel 34:7–16 is part of a series of messages that speak about the fall of Jerusalem. The destruction is the outcome of the nation violating the covenant (see Deut. 28:49–52, 63–65). This portion is clearly addressed to the "shepherds" of the people: **Therefore, you shepherds, hear the word of the Lord** (v. 7). Today we usually think of a shepherd of the flock as a pastor over a congregation. However Ezekiel's meaning is a bit different. Primarily he was referring to the king, his nobles, and the political leaders of the community. Leaders and kings were often referred to as **shepherds** (see Isa. 44:28, where King Cyrus of Persia is called a "shepherd"). Two of the greatest leaders of Israel are called shepherds: Moses (Isa. 63:11) and David (Ps. 78:70–72). What is fascinating is that God called both of these leaders while they were tending sheep.

The basic charge against the shepherds is that they have ceased to shepherd. Although they have positions of leadership, they have concentrated on the privileges and ignored their responsibilities. As shepherds, their primary job was to protect and provide for the people. Instead of being protectors, they were predators; and instead of providing, they were parasites. The charges are fleshed out in the first six verses of Ezekiel 34. They were accused of three things: cruel exploitation (vv. 2–3), not giving care to the weak (v. 4), and scattering the flock (vv. 5–6). Because the shepherds have ignored their obligations, the flock **has been plundered and has become food for all the wild animals** (v. 8). Instead of gathering the flock together and protecting it from danger, the shepherds **cared for themselves**. As long as there are leaders, this is a danger. When the Israelites asked for a king in the days of Samuel, the elders making the request focused on the benefits that a king can bring: "to go out before us and fight our battles" (1 Sam. 8:20). Samuel warned them that a king would want to take sons, daughters, land, produce, and livestock until they would "cry out for relief" (8:10–18). It is certainly possible for a king to put his responsibilities first, but the sad histories of most kings show how rare this is.

---

## WORDS FROM WESLEY
### *Ezekiel 34:7*

*The shepherds*—The rulers of the people, kings, magistrates, and princes; as also priests, and prophets. (ENOT, Ezek. 34:2)

---

The excesses of the leaders lead to the Lord saying, **"I am against the shepherds and will hold them accountable for my flock. I will remove them"** (v. 10). Notice that while earlier God said the flock had become food for wild animals, now it is the pseudo-shepherds who are pictured as eating the flock. They are some of the wild animals from which the flock needs protection!

The picture is that of snatching prey from the jaws of predators just as the jaws are about to snap shut.

## To Sheep Who Suffered under the "Shepherds" (Ezek. 34:11–16)

For the fourth time since verse 7 we have an announcement that this message is from the Lord. The previous paragraph ended with the notice that God would remove the exploiting shepherds and rescue His flock. Now we hear that the Lord himself will become the shepherd. No longer will God appoint under-shepherds, but He will assume direct responsibility for the welfare of His sheep: **"I *myself* will . . . look after them"** (v. 11, emphasis added).

Seventeen statements in only six verses assure the flock of God's care! Notice that two verbs are repeated: "look after" and "to tend." These are exactly the things the false shepherds failed to do. The false shepherds only looked after and tended themselves at the expense of the sheep.

---

### WORDS FROM WESLEY

*Ezekiel 34:12*

God, whose mercies never end,
Thy gracious promise keep,
Raise the Shepherd up, and send
To seek the wandering sheep,
A lost race to save and feed
When in one fold together join'd,
Join'd in spirit to our Head
The Shepherd of mankind.
The true heavenly David give,
The just and loving One,
After Thine own heart, to live,
And fix in us His throne:
When on every soul bestow'd,
He comes, and saves us from our sins,
Father, then Thou art our God,
And Jesus is our Prince. (PW, vol. 10, 54)

---

The flock had been scattered. It was no longer in the best pastureland. It had no protection from wild beasts. When the Lord tends His sheep, all these are reversed. God searches for, rescues, gathers, and places the sheep in the best of the land. Besides the verbs describing God's action, note that the next most common theme is that the sheep will be in **their own land . . . on the mountains of Israel, in the ravines and in all the settlements in the land . . . in a good pasture, and the mountain heights of Israel will be their grazing land. There they will lie down in good grazing land, and there they will feed in a rich pasture on the mountains of Israel** (vv. 13–14). It is difficult to think of stronger terms to describe God's actions and its results.

There is one puzzling phrase in the list—**"I will destroy"** (v. 16). Why is this negative action mentioned? Notice that the full phrase is **"the sleek and strong I will destroy." The sleek and strong** are the shepherds who have gotten that way from exploiting the flock. This is followed by the concluding sentence: **"I will shepherd the flock with justice."** God remembers and will deal with those who exploit others for their own gain.

### The Great Shepherd Is Coming (Jer. 23:1–6)

Jeremiah's words from the Lord were most likely delivered a bit before the words of Ezekiel above. The immediate audiences of the two prophets were also different. Ezekiel spoke to those already in exile about the final destruction of their homeland and its eventual rebuilding. Jeremiah, on the other hand, spoke to people in Judah who were direct participants in those last days. The emphasis is also slightly different. Both prophets highlighted the faults of the current shepherds and also that God had not forgotten His sheep. Ezekiel has a great deal to say about the *what* of God's action, while Jeremiah speaks more about the *who*.

**Woe to the shepherds** (v. 1). Like Ezekiel, Jeremiah began with an indictment against the rulers of Judah. The word **woe**, also translated "alas," is used to express great sorrow (Jer. 22:13, 18). Mourners in a funeral procession frequently used it. Prophets used it to both express sorrow at the current state of affairs and also to announce coming judgment. Think of it as introducing a "this is your funeral" message.

Just as Ezekiel emphasized that he was delivering a message from the Lord, here in these six verses we see five affirmations that Jeremiah was not delivering a personal opinion or private bias, but he spoke for the Lord. The charges against the shepherds are similar to what we have already seen. They are **destroying and scattering the sheep** (23:1). They have **driven them away and have not bestowed care on them** (v. 2). God's response to the neglect and exploitation of the sheep closely fits the offense. Because the shepherds **have not *bestowed* care on them, I will *bestow* punishment** (emphasis added).

God's response goes beyond just removing and punishing the false shepherds: **I myself will gather the remnant of my flock** (v. 3). Not only will the scattered flock be returned to their own space (**pasture**), but also they will prosper. **They will be fruitful and increase in number** echoes the blessing God gave at creation (see Gen. 1:28).

While both Ezekiel and Jeremiah emphasize that God himself will be personally and directly involved in restoring the flock, Jeremiah went on to say that the false shepherds will be replaced by good. It is in this context that Jeremiah saw a time of restoration under the Messiah, a descendant of **David, a righteous Branch** (v. 5). God does not forget His covenants. In 2 Samuel 7, God made a covenant with David and told him, "I took you from the pasture and from following the flock to be ruler over my people Israel" (v. 8). Then God makes the promise, "Your house and your kingdom will endure forever before me; your throne will be established forever" (v. 16).

All these threads come together in the person of Jesus Christ, who is both divine and human. As a man He is a descendant of

David; as God He personally cares for His flock. When Jesus says, "I am the good shepherd" (John 10:11, 14) or that His mission was "to seek and to save what was lost" (Luke 19:10), it is hard to miss the connection with the words of Ezekiel and Jeremiah.

---

### WORDS FROM WESLEY

*Jeremiah 23:5*

*Behold*—Even the Jewish doctors, as well as the Christian interpreters, understand this as a prophecy of the Messiah who is called the branch, Isa. 4:2, 53:2. And here He is called the righteous branch, not only because himself was righteous, but because He maketh His people righteous. *Shall execute*—Protecting the innocent, and defending His people throughout the world, judging the prince of the world, and by His spirit governing His people. (ENOT)

---

Jeremiah closed his words about the King God is sending by announcing His name: **The Lord Our Righteousness** (v. 6). This is a deliberate play on the name of the last king who ruled before Babylon conquered Judah. His throne name was Zedekiah, which means "my righteousness is the Lord," but he did not live up to that name. God's promised King switches the name around and now the emphasis is the Lord is our righteousness. The coming King will not just have the name, but will live up to it. Wisdom, justice, and righteousness characterize His reign. In the book of Revelation, John summed up the outcome: "For the Lamb at the center of the throne will be their shepherd; he will lead them to springs of living water. And God will wipe away every tear from their eyes" (Rev. 7:17).

●

## WORDS FROM WESLEY

*Jeremiah 23:6*

One very considerable article of this truth is contained in the words above recited, "This is his name whereby he shall be called, the Lord our righteousness"; a truth this, which enters deep into the nature of Christianity, and, in a manner, supports the whole frame of it. Of this, undoubtedly, may be affirmed, what Luther affirms of a truth closely connected with it. . . . The Christian church stands or falls with it. It is certainly the pillar and ground of that faith, of which alone cometh salvation; of that Catholic or universal faith which is found in all the children of God, and which "unless a man keep whole and undefiled, without doubt he shall perish everlastingly." (WJW, vol. 5, 235)

## DISCUSSION

List some qualities of a good leader. List some qualities of a self-centered leader.

1. In what ways can leaders be compared with shepherds? In what ways can people be compared with sheep?

2. List the reasons Ezekiel gave for God's anger toward the rulers.

3. The people demanded a king. What effect did it produce in their lives when they ceased to be ruled by God and were ruled by a man?

4. Is it possible for a church (or community) to be righteous without the leadership of godly people? Explain.

5. What factors might cause a leader who begins with good motives to lose sight of his or her purpose?

6. List several reasons why it is important to pray for national leaders, regardless of whether they are godly.

7. If great personal sacrifice were the price of being an effective leader, would you still sign up for the job? Explain.

8. In what ways could you both support and hold accountable those who are in leadership over you?

9. How will your personal faith in God affect future generations?

## PRAYER

Lord, bless those who are in authority with a spirit of service and humility before You.

# NEW HOPE

*Ezekiel 37:1–14*

---

God brings new life to hopeless people.

*Dead*. It is a word void of possibility. We often apply it to circumstances in which we see no hope. When there is no way out, we are at a dead end. When a marriage seems to be beyond saving, we say that the relationship is dead. When a congregation is in danger of disbanding, we say that the church died.

Perhaps there is a situation in your life that you would describe as dead.

This study reminds us that when God is involved, there is no situation that is beyond hope. Although we might think of our circumstances as dead, God can breathe new life into them. This study will set your sights on what is possible through faith.

## COMMENTARY

When the full weight of God's judgment fell on Judah and the survivors went into exile in Babylonia, they apparently slipped into a severe depression regarding any further hope for the nation, convinced their violation of the covenant was so severe that they would never again experience the blessings of the covenant and promises. They had no hope for a future with God.

It is precisely this despair that this vision in Ezekiel addresses. Whereas the people had no hope, God was giving them a radical new perspective of a future filled with hope.

**Vision Report (Ezek. 37:1–10)**

Ezekiel 37:1–14 is the famous "vision of the dry bones," and divides into two main parts: (1) the vision itself (vv. 1–10), and (2) the interpretation of the vision (vv. 11–14).

Note that the vision (metaphor) occurs first, and only then does the interpretation follow. Too frequently we jump to the interpretation (bones equals Judah or Israel) and read the vision in light of that interpretation. But by so doing, we "debone" the vision of its impact.

The vision itself consists of four sections.

*1. Indication of the Experience as a Vision (Ezek. 37:1).* Ezekiel's experience is clearly indicated as a vision by the introductory phrase **the hand of the LORD was upon me** (v. 1). Although we at times use similar language to indicate a special sense of the presence of God, in Ezekiel, this phrase is technical language that specifically and exclusively refers to having a visionary experience from God. Every vision in the book of Ezekiel employs this language to describe it.

The phrase **and he brought me out by the Spirit of the LORD** (v. 1) also indicates the visionary nature of this experience. When used elsewhere in Ezekiel, this phrase refers to the prophet being set on his feet so as to receive the revelatory word in the midst of a vision or to the transportation from one location to another within the visionary experience. However, here in 37:1, he was brought out only within the vision. His body remained in the same place throughout the vision.

*2. Description of the Visual Imagery (Ezek. 37:1–2).* In the vision, Ezekiel was transported to **the middle of a valley** that **was full of bones** (v. 1). Ezekiel recounted in the first person: **He led me back and forth among them, and I saw a great many bones on the floor of the valley, bones that were very dry** (v. 2).

Two things are emphasized about the bones: first, the massive amount of them, and second, their dryness. In other words, the picture is that of a vast number of people who have perished quite some time before, since the flesh has had time to decay or be picked clean by animals, and the bones had become bleached by the elements.

Another aspect of the imagery here is a sense of the shameful nature of the death. In ancient Near Eastern culture, proper burial was considered a social requirement, so a body being left out and exposed to the animals and elements without a proper burial was a matter of humiliation.

---

### WORDS FROM WESLEY

*Ezekiel 37:1*

*And set me down*—So it seemed to me in the vision. Which is a lively representation of a threefold resurrection: (1) Of the resurrection of souls, from the death of sin, to the life of righteousness; (2) the resurrection of the church from an afflicted state, to liberty and peace; (3) the resurrection of the body at the great day, especially the bodies of believers to life eternal. (ENOT)

---

Although not explicit, implied is that Ezekiel came upon the aftermath of the defeat of a massive army that had been left where they fell in battle. Verse 9 says they were "slain," and verse 10 notes that when the bones were revived, they "stood up on their feet—a vast army." The battle imagery fits well when we understand that the bones refer to the "whole house of Israel" (v. 11), for it was in the context of battling with the Babylonians that Judah had been slain.

*3. Dialogue: God's Question and Ezekiel's Response (Ezek. 37:3).* After Ezekiel had seen the vastness and dryness of the bones, God asked him, **"Son of man, can these bones live?"** (v. 3). Given the context of living following the resurrection of Jesus and having an understanding of the resurrection of the dead at the end times, we would undoubtedly respond with a resounding yes. But Ezekiel didn't have our historical perspective. At that time, even though there was a clear belief in some type of shadowy existence after death, there was yet no broad affirmation of a general resurrection from the dead. Thus God was asking Ezekiel whether He can do the radical, inconceivable, impossible, and even the unbelievable.

Ezekiel's answer— **"O Sovereign Lord, you alone know"**— neither affirms nor denies. Although Ezekiel would affirm that God *could* do anything, even the impossible, the issue may be more whether God wills to bring the bones back to life. God executed the judgment that produced these bones in the first place. So even though God has the power and capability of bringing the bones back to life, is this what He *wants* to do with them? Also at this point in the vision, God had not yet expressed any intent for the bones, so Ezekiel did not know what God willed to do. Thus his response expressed faith in God without dictating to God what He must do.

*4. Twofold Sequence of Bringing the Bones to Life (Ezek. 37:4–10).* Verses 4–10 follow a twofold sequence of (1) a command to prophesy followed by (2) a report that the prophet did such, and then the passage concludes with the results of the prophesying.

Immediately after the first command to **prophesy** (v. 4), God expressed what He intended to do to the bones: **"I will make breath enter you, and you will come to life"** (v. 5). He emphasized this intent by stating it twice (vv. 5–6).

In this first sequence, we are again positioned right alongside Ezekiel, experiencing the events as he did. So we can almost hear **a noise, a rattling sound** (v. 7), and our amazement is heightened as we experience the outworking of the divine intent: **the bones came together, bone to bone**.

Our expectations of complete fulfillment are raised as Ezekiel prophesied to the bones as commanded, and **tendons and flesh appeared on them and skin covered them** (v. 8).

---

### WORDS FROM WESLEY

*Ezekiel 37:4*

Hear ye dry bones, and feel
The word of truth and grace:
I will in you Myself reveal,
I will your spirits raise;
(Jehovah speaks the word,)
The promise is for you,
Ye shall be gradually restored,
And fashion'd all anew:
Cover'd with flesh and skin
Ye shall your Saviour know,
And find the breath of life within,
Which I on all bestow:
The joyful news receive,
The grace to sinners given,
The knowledge of your Lord, and live
The sinless life of heaven. (PW, vol. 10, 59–60)

---

However, the abruptness of verse 8—**but there was no breath in them**—stops us in our tracks, because this was *not* the divine intent. And because **there was no breath in them**, the result intended in verses 5 and 6 (**and you will come to life**) also did not occurred.

---

### WORDS FROM WESLEY

*Ezekiel 37:7*

*Came together*—Glided nearer and nearer, 'till each bone met the bone to which it was to be joined. Of all the bones of all those numerous slain, not one was missing not one missed its way not one missed its place, but each knew and found its fellow. Thus in the resurrection of the dead, the scattered atoms shall be arranged in their proper place and order, and every bone *come to his bone*, by the same wisdom and power by which they were first formed in the womb of her that is with child. (ENOT)

---

The second sequence (vv. 9–10) rectifies that lack. But the question arises as to why the twofold sequence; why was not the whole accomplished in one act?

The twofold sequence seems to serve two functions. The moving toward fulfillment experienced in verses 7–8 is abruptly halted by the fact that **there was no breath in them**. That hesitation in the movement helps to highlight the miraculous nature of what finally occurs. The effect is similar to the use of slow motion in movies. Just as the runner is rushing toward the finish line, the motion is slowed to heighten the anticipation and one is forced to think about the expected outcome. With the words of verse 8, the question arises: Is this too difficult for God? But when the events of verse 10 occur, the miraculous nature of what has transpired is highlighted. This was no easy task, yet God performed it.

The other reason for the twofold sequence deals with the imagery. The sequence of first constructing the bodies with the bones covered with flesh, and then filling those bodies with breath and life is the same sequence that occurs in the creation of the human in Genesis 2:7. Step 1: "The Lord God formed the man from the dust of the ground . . ." Step 2: "and breathed into his nostrils the breath of life . . ." Result: "and the man became a living being."

Although the allusion to Genesis 2:7 is clear, it must be noted that different terms are used: *breath* in Ezekiel 37 is not the same Hebrew term as *breath of life* in Genesis 2, and *life* in Ezekiel 37 is not the same term as *a living being* in Genesis 2. Still, the sequence in Ezekiel 37 is a clear allusion to the creation imagery, and the restoration prophesied in verses 12–14 can be understood as "new creation" imagery.

Because there was no breath in them, Ezekiel was commanded again to **prophesy** (v. 9), but now **to the breath**, telling it to **come from the four winds . . . and breathe into these slain, that they may live.**

As a result, **breath entered them; they came to life** (v. 10). Now the dry bones have become a living, **vast army**. The language here is reminiscent of the descriptions of the Israelites as they left Egypt, indicating that this "new exodus" from this exile must be compared to the first one. Also, the vastness of the people indicates a re-experiencing of the fulfillment of God's promise to Abraham that he would become a vast nation, a reversal of the recent decimation of the population by the Babylonians.

## The Interpretation (Ezek. 37:11–14)

A brief statement—**these bones are the whole house of Israel** (v. 11)—clarifies the subject of the vision.

Just as the bones are described in verses 1–2, so too the whole house of Israel as bones is described in verse 11: **Our bones are dried up and our hope is gone; we are cut off**. The people's self-assessment drips with hopelessness. The phrase **we are cut off** primarily refers to exclusion and separation, and frequently carries the connotation of death. But it can also mean being excluded and separated from the presence of God. Thus from the people's perspective, they had violated the covenant and were suffering the consequences of judgment, which meant the death of the nation and an irrevocable severance of the covenant relationship with God.

Through the vision, God reassured His people. Even though they were bones and had been put to death, they would not remain that way forever, because God was going to do a radical, unexpected, even impossible work.

The vision of the dry bones is a picture of the reviving of the nations of Judah and Israel, which will involve three elements: (1) bringing them up from the nations in which they are exiled; (2) restoring them to the Promised Land; and (3) putting His Spirit in them with the result that they will live.

---

## WORDS FROM WESLEY

### Ezekiel 37:12

*I will open*—Though your captivity be as death, your persons close as the grave, yet I will open those graves. (ENOT)

---

This whole prophecy is couched in terms of what God would do. The initiative was God's, and there was no indication that the restoration from exile was a divine response to the people repenting from their sin. It was an act of divine grace and mercy to a people who were suffering the full results for their violation of the covenant. The result, then, of God's activity was that the people were to recognize Him.

The point of this passage is that God was doing the inconceivable amid a hopeless situation. Whereas the people were discouraged, and corporately dead and dismembered, they ended up reunited and revived. If we get hung up on trying to determine a historical fulfillment of when this happened, we may very well overlook the truth that this is one of the ongoing ways in which God works with His people, the church. A local church may be virtually "dead," yet God may want to raise it back to life. A chastised, disciplined Christian may feel like he or she has no hope of a close relationship with God ever being restored; yet God may want to restore that person to both an intimacy of relationship as well as to a place of service.

## DISCUSSION

Share about what happened the last time you were forced out of your comfort zone and how it made you feel.

1. Do you think Ezekiel's vision describes a physical or spiritual resurrection or both? Explain.

2. What do you think was the purpose of the resurrected army Ezekiel envisioned?

3. Why did God ask Ezekiel to speak to the bones instead of just doing it himself?

4. In what ways could a person or church be like the dry bones Ezekiel saw?

5. What would breathe new life into a spiritually dead person or community?

6. What actions could we take to facilitate such an event?

7. Do you think some people are so spiritually dead they can never be reborn?

8. What would your life be like if you received a fresh breath of the Spirit?

9. What do you think God could accomplish in your community if there was a dramatic spiritual awakening in your church?

## PRAYER

Let the Holy Spirit come and take control and send a great revival in our souls!

## 10

# THE POWER OF INTEGRITY

*Daniel 1:8–20*

---

We maintain integrity by focusing on God
rather than our circumstances.

All of us face the pressure to conform. We like to fit in at work. We dislike standing out in a crowd. We want to be liked. Following Christ faithfully, however, will require us to maintain a distinction between ourselves and the way of the world. As Paul advised in Romans 12:1, we must not allow the world to squeeze us into its mold. That isn't easy. From choices in entertainment to sexual morality to ethics in business, we continually face the pressure, subtle or overt, to behave as nonbelievers do.

This study will give you strength and confidence to maintain your integrity as a follower of Christ and to trust God regardless of the pressures around you.

## COMMENTARY

The year was 605 B.C. The fall of Jerusalem and the exile of the general populace to Babylon wouldn't take place for another nineteen years, but the process had already begun. Daniel 1:1–2 reports that "in the third year of the reign of Jehoiakim king of Judah," Judah lay helpless as Nebuchadnezzar sacked Jerusalem, taking many of the nobles and people of importance captive to Babylon (among them Daniel, Shadrach, Meshach, and Abednego). But it wasn't just the result of political upheaval and conquering armies. It was the judgment of God on an arrogant and defiant people. It was a warning of what was to come. God's judgment on the sin of the nation was coming to fruition.

Daniel 1:8–20 shows Daniel and his three friends standing in sharp contrast to the apostate and immoral people of Judah. They were taken captive as "casualties of war." That is, they suffered because of the sin of the nation even though they themselves were not the object of God's anger and judgment. They serve as a reminder that God always preserved a faithful "remnant" who remained righteous and godly even in the midst of a decadent society. It is also a reminder that God is gracious and faithful to those who are faithful to Him. All through the book of Daniel we see these righteous men standing firm for God, and God vindicating them and proving His faithfulness. Although Daniel is among the first to be taken captive, he outlives his captors and their empire (5:29–31).

Some commentators have compared the story of Daniel to that of Moses and the Israelites' flight from Egypt. At that pivotal point in Israel's history, God proved to a pagan nation that the God of Israel was more powerful than the gods of Egypt (Num. 33:4). Now again, centuries later, to a pagan nation that believes the fate of battles lies in the hands of the respective gods, the Lord God must show unequivocally that He is more powerful than the gods of Babylon. His people weren't captured because the Babylonian gods were stronger, but because it was God's will to punish them in such a way. The story of Daniel serves as a reminder to all the nations of who is really God.

Daniel 1 sets the background for this first story. The brightest, most handsome, and most qualified of the Israelite captives were brought into the king's palace to learn the language and literature of the Babylonians. They were to be assimilated into the culture and treated like royalty, with the eventual prospect of entering into the king's service. Their names were changed, a common practice of subjugation. We see no indication of resistance on the part of any of the Israelite natives, save Daniel, Shadrach, Meshach, and Abednego.

## Daniel's Resolve (Dan. 1:8–10)

**Daniel resolved not to defile himself with the royal food and wine** (v. 8). Some believe that since the first portion of the king's food and wine were offered to idols or poured out on pagan altars, Daniel objected to taking the food and wine on religious grounds— he did not want to be a willing participant to their idolatry. Others believe the animals offered may have been ceremonially unclean (perhaps strangled instead of having the blood drained, or simply animals classified as "unclean" in the Levitical law and therefore prohibited; see Ex. 34:15), and Daniel did not want to break the dietary laws found in the Pentateuch. But his reasons were probably much deeper. Daniel's homeland was under siege. His people were experiencing the brunt of God's wrath. Poverty and widespread famine were likely. How could Daniel dine on the king's food and wine when his compatriots were devastated? It would seem almost treasonous. In the ancient Near East, to share a meal with a man signified a commitment to friendship and fellowship. It was an honor not taken lightly. In this case, the king was looking for loyalty and service from these captives, and partaking of the king's food was a way of acknowledging loyalty to him and committing to a friendly relationship with him. How could Daniel possibly defile himself in such a way as to join hands with the enemy of Judah? How could he betray his fellow Israelites by eating the king's food at his table?

Fittingly, Daniel resolved (he decided ahead of time, before the opportunity presented itself) not to take the king's food but to eat only what was necessary for subsistence. This same word used for *resolved* is also found in 11:17 (where the king of the North will "determine" to come and make an alliance with the king of the South) and in 6:17 (where a stone was "placed" over the mouth of the den of lions). Daniel's resolve was as immovable as a mighty empire or a sealed stone, a testimony to the strength and forcefulness of his commitment to God and his determination to do what was right. Every Christian would be wise to heed his example. God will do great things in and through the believer who has made such a commitment, a commitment to be faithful no matter what the cost.

---

## WORDS FROM WESLEY
### *Daniel 1:8*

The lowest kind of fasting, if it can be called by that name, is the abstaining from pleasant food. Of this, we have several instances in Scripture, besides that of Daniel and his brethren, who from a peculiar consideration, namely, that they might "not defile themselves with the portion of the King's meat, nor with the wine which he drank" (a daily provision of which the King had appointed for them), requested and obtained, of the prince of the eunuchs, pulse to eat and water to drink (Dan. 1:8). Perhaps from a mistaken imitation of this might spring the very ancient custom of abstaining from flesh and wine during such times as were set apart for fasting and abstinence—if it did not rather arise from a supposition that these were the most pleasant food, and a belief that it was proper to use what was least pleasing at those times of solemn approach to God. (WJW, vol. 5, 347)

---

But Daniel was not a fool. He did not brazenly defy the king's command or make a fuss in front of the other captives. Instead, he quietly **asked the chief official for permission not to defile himself in this way** (1:8). He didn't demand. He didn't pontificate or insult his overseers. He simply requested permission. He lived out Peter's admonition in 1 Peter 3:15: "But in your hearts set apart Christ as Lord. Always be prepared to give an answer to everyone who asks you to give the reason for the hope that you have. But do this with gentleness and respect."

There is no doubt that God had guided Daniel in how to approach the chief official, Ashpenaz. God was already working in the situation. **Now God had caused the official to show favor**

**and sympathy to Daniel** (Dan. 1:9). Just as Joseph had found favor before Potiphar (Gen. 39:2–4), the prison warden (39:21), and the pharaoh (41:16, 41–43), so Daniel found favor in Babylon. But even though there was some type of close relationship between Daniel and Ashpenaz, fear kept him from granting Daniel's request. **Why should** the king **see you looking worse than the other young men your age? The king would then have my head because of you** (Dan 1:10). His concern was legitimate. These men had been placed under his care to be trained to serve the king. It wouldn't do to have Daniel and his friends looking undernourished and sluggish. Surely the king would blame Ashpenaz for failing to carry out his duty. But Daniel had a plan.

---

### WORDS FROM WESLEY

*Daniel 1:8*

*But Daniel purposed*—There may be several weighty reasons assigned why Daniel did this. (1) Because many of those meats provided for the king's table, were forbidden by the Jewish law. (2) Daniel knew these delicates would too much gratify the flesh. (3) He did not dare to eat and drink things consecrated to idols. (4) He was sensible, how unsuitable delicate fare would be to the afflicted state of God's people. Therefore he was herein a rare pattern of avoiding all the occasions of evil. (ENOT)

---

### Daniel's Risk (Dan. 1:11–16)

Daniel didn't want to endanger his Babylonian friend, but he wanted to be faithful to the conviction God had placed on his heart. So he decided to take a risk. He approached **the guard whom the chief official had appointed** (v. 11) over him and his friends with a proposition, a test: **for ten days . . . give us nothing but vegetables to eat and water to drink** (v. 12). The period of time was short enough that no lasting damage could be done, but long enough to prove Daniel's point. He put the outcome in the guard's hand: **Then compare our appearance with that of the young men who eat the royal food, and treat your servants in accordance with what you see** (v. 13). The word translated in the NIV as vegetables (*hazeraim*) means seeds or grain, herbs or garden plants. He wasn't asking for a lush diet of the best vegetables, which we would expect to make him healthier, but a diet of simple grains and seeds (maybe including whatever fruit might have been in season). It was a meager diet. Daniel was taking a risk. He was putting his trust in God.

This was Daniel's first exercise of real faith that would prepare him for even greater challenges in the future. Oftentimes God uses small obstacles (and what might appear to be small successes) to prepare us and strengthen us for future trials. Here Daniel learned to trust God in the area of food (where the consequences may have been merely physical punishment); later he would need to trust God as he prayed under the threat of the lions' den. It is interesting how many Christians will compromise on the little things, thinking them unimportant, but claim they will never waver in the "big" things. But one is the preparation for the other. Faith and obedience are developed over the long haul.

The guard could hardly refuse Daniel's request and consequently **tested them for ten days** (v. 14). According to the *Pulpit Commentary* (vol. 29, p. 22), ancient reliefs of another Babylonian king's feast show the guests seated in groups of four around small tables, not all around one large banquet table as we often picture in our minds. Since Daniel and his three friends numbered four, no doubt they sat together at meals and could have easily concealed their strange diet from the other captives or their captors. Since, after the test was over and the guard was convinced, he **took away their choice food and the wine they were to drink and gave them vegetables instead** (v. 16), it is highly probable that the guard brought them the king's food every day for the entire ten days, and only took it away at their request. The verb tense used for "took" away indicates this was a customary practice. Every day they had to make the decision again to not defile themselves. After ten days of seeds and grain, a sumptuous meal of meat and wine placed on the table in front of them would have been tempting indeed—especially since no one else knew of their vow. But God always gives strength amid temptation and enables us to obey (1 Cor. 10:13).

Daniel took a risk and God was proved faithful. **At the end of the ten days they looked healthier and better nourished than any of the young men who ate the royal food** (Dan. 1:15).

---

### WORDS FROM WESLEY

*Daniel 1:15*

*Fairer and fatter*—The blessing of God upon homely fare, affords often more health and strength, than more costly fare to them that eat the fat, and drink the sweet. (ENOT)

---

### Daniel's Reward (Dan. 1:17–20)

God rewarded Daniel, Shadrach, Meshach, and Abednego for their commitment to Him, just as He had rewarded Joseph in Genesis 41. He **gave** them **knowledge and understanding . . . and Daniel could understand visions and dreams of all kinds** (Dan. 1:17). Daniel 2:17–28 makes it clear that the meanings of dreams were revealed to him by God, highlighting again the faithfulness of God to His true followers even amid the most trying times.

When Daniel and his friends were **presented** to **Nebuchadnezzar** (v. 18) at the end of their three years of training, the king (possibly after talking to them about his dream of ch. 2) **found none equal to Daniel, Hannaniah, Mishael and Azariah** (v. 19). God didn't just keep them from harm during these three years of captivity, He made them excel. **In every matter of wisdom and understanding about which the king questioned them, he found them ten times better than all the magicians and enchanters in his whole kingdom** (v. 20). Our God is bigger than the god of this world. Those who practiced the occult were no match for the power of an almighty God.

---

### WORDS FROM WESLEY

*Daniel 1:20*

*The king enquired—*This is a farther confirmation of the king's noble endowments, and of his great care whom he chose to be in offices of trust, namely persons excellently qualified to serve him in the great affairs of the kingdom. And thus did God pour contempt upon the pride of the Chaldeans, and put honour on the low estate of his people. (ENOT)

---

Daniel continued to be faithful to the Lord throughout his life, and God's reward also continued (see 2:48–49; 5:29). Of this we can be certain: "He who sows righteousness reaps a sure reward" (Prov. 11:18).

# DISCUSSION

Share which is harder for you to resist and why: the pressure to blend in with the crowd or the urge to get attention.

1. The king's diet was designed to make Daniel healthier. What were his reasons for not following it?

2. What factors might have made it difficult for Daniel to insist on following his principles?

3. We often think of biblical men and women as superheroes, but they were ordinary people just like us. Describe the emotions Daniel might have felt during this experience.

4. Why do you think God would allow Daniel to remain a captive even after he had shown such courage by being obedient?

5. Why do you think some temptations seem to affect people differently?

6. What spiritual resources were available to Daniel that might have enabled him to stand firm? What spiritual resources are available to you?

7. Does God still offer supernatural wisdom and guidance to us today? If so, how?

8. Can you think of a time you received extraordinary strength in the midst of a hardship? Explain.

9. If your life were a boxing match—flesh versus Spirit—which opponent would be winning right now?

# PRAYER

Lord, cleanse us and we will be clean.

# 11

# LEARNING TO TRUST GOD

*Daniel 3:1, 4–6, 12–28*

Choosing to trust God always produces the best result.

Many of us would be hard pressed to think of a person so filled with hostility toward us that we would call him or her an enemy. Yet many brothers and sisters in Christ around the world regularly face enemies of the gospel—and are persecuted or even martyred as a result. Closer to home, we may live in tension with those who, though not violent, would wish us harm. How do you respond when others oppose you or aim to prevent you from doing what is right? How do you peacefully coexist with those who think ill of you?

This study offers good advice for those who deal with enemies, either across the ocean or across the street. You will gain courage and confidence to trust God and do what is right in spite of those who may oppose you.

## COMMENTARY

The famous, or infamous, Nebuchadnezzar ruled as king of Babylon for forty-three years, from 604 to 562 B.C. He is responsible for transforming Babylon into the greatest city of the ancient world. Today, the city's ruins spread over two thousand acres, making it far and away the largest city anywhere in that part of the world. One of the city's most dazzling sites was the wall around the city's perimeter, a wall that could be entered only by eight gates, each named after a god.

Inside the city, Nebuchadnezzar supervised some magnificent building projects. Among the more celebrated of these was a seven-staged brick temple-tower whose height may have reached three hundred feet. The Babylonian name for this structure translates as "house of the foundation of heaven and earth," suggesting, perhaps, some parallel function with the city-tower story recorded in Genesis 11:1–9.

Other magnificent structures include numerous temples, possibly as many as fifty, and especially his own royal palace. We do not know for sure whether Nebuchadnezzar himself built the famous Hanging Gardens of Babylon. He never alluded to these gardens in the many inscriptions archaeologists have discovered from his era. It is later authors who connect these gardens with this Babylonian king.

The Old Testament records Nebuchadnezzar invading Judah and Jerusalem three times. The first took place in 606 B.C., the third year of the reign of Jehoiakim in Jerusalem. This was actually before Nebuchadnezzar commenced his reign. At this time, he was still the crown prince who had taken command of the army of his father, Nabopolasser, possibly because of his father's advanced age or poor health. This was the occasion on which Daniel and his friends were captured and carried to Babylon (see Dan. 1:1), although Nebuchadnezzar in his own records never referred to this particular siege.

He attacked Jerusalem again in 597 B.C. (see 2 Kings 24:1–17). Yet a third time he laid siege against Jerusalem, which fell to the invader between 587 and 586 B.C. (see 2 Kings 25:1–26). The thoroughness of his devastation of Jerusalem and surrounding cities can be gauged by the fact that archaeological evidence suggests that the population of Judah fell from a quarter of a million in the eighth century B.C. to half that after the fall of Jerusalem during this time.

### Nebuchadnezzar's Image (Dan. 3:1)

Nebuchadnezzar's **image** is one he made of **gold** (v. 1), which may mean either pure gold or gold-plated. The Aramaic word for *image* is the same as that used in Genesis 1 for God's creation of human beings. God made humankind in His image, and Nebuchadnezzar made an image. If God made an image to reflect himself and His glory, did Nebuchadnezzar also make an image to reflect himself and his glory? We cannot be certain whether the image was intended to represent Nebuchadnezzar himself or one of his Babylonian gods, or just the golden era of his reign.

The location of the image's site, **Dura**, is uncertain, for many places were called "Dura," but we do know that the dimensions of the image, **ninety feet high and nine feet wide**, are hard to envision. The fact that the height is ten times greater than the width makes this pole-like, top-heavy statue a golden monstrosity.

---

### WORDS FROM WESLEY

*Daniel 3:1*

*Made an image*—Perhaps he did this, that he might seem no ways inclined to the Jews, or their religion, whereof the Chaldeans might be jealous, seeing he had owned their God to be greatest, and had preferred Daniel and his friends to great honours. (ENOT)

---

## All Must Worship the Image (Dan. 3:4–6)

To the setting of **music** (v. 5), which often is still a part of and prelude to state and religious processions and ceremonies, all present on this occasion were commanded to **fall down and worship** the image. In so doing, the audience was not so much engaging in a religious act as they were swearing allegiance to the king.

One way this is brought out is by the fact that seven times in the chapter (vv. 2, 3, 5, 7, 12, 14, 18) we are told that the image was one Nebuchadnezzar himself "had set up." Such obvious repetition draws attention to the fact that the real importance of the image lies in who crafted it.

The consequence for refusing to worship this image was that any nonconformists would **immediately be thrown into a blazing furnace** (v. 6). So, by threatening burning, Nebuchadnezzar sought to control the behavior of this group of people.

This furnace would have been a kiln-type oven, beehive shaped, with openings or doors on the top and at ground level. It could be heated in excess of two thousand degrees Fahrenheit.

### Three Jews Rejected the Order (Dan. 3:12)

We do not know where Daniel was at this time. Was he traveling elsewhere? Did he pretend to bow? Or did his high office in the administration (see 2:48) give him a certain immunity from the charges brought by the astrologers against his three fellows?

It is important to note how the accusers crafted their indictment. They did not say, "These individuals have ignored the decree" or the like. Instead, they made Nebuchadnezzar the target of the affront by repeatedly using **you** and **your: Jews whom *you* have set over the affairs . . . who pay no attention to *you* . . . neither serve *your* gods nor worship the image of gold *you* have set up** (v. 12, emphasis added). In other words, the act of defiance is not so much political or religious betrayal as it is personal betrayal. These three Jews were really backstabbers, so suggested the prosecutors.

### There Is One More Chance to Conform (Dan. 3:13–15)

Nebuchadnezzar had a problem both with pride and anger. Often the two go together, especially when arrogance is challenged. It is somewhat understandable why he was **furious with rage** (v. 13), or just "furious" (v. 19), and that is because the nonconformists who trusted in the Lord were, therefore, beyond the king's ability to intimidate. For a powerful person to lose the power of intimidation is for that person to surrender one of his most lethal weapons.

We need to give Nebuchadnezzar a little bit of credit here. He did not accept the astrologers' charges unquestioningly. He summoned the three Jews before him and allowed them to state their own position. At the same time, he betrayed his true colors by saying sarcastically at the end, **"what god will be able to rescue you from my hand?"** (v. 15). It was difficult for Nebuchadnezzar to believe that there was any force greater than he operating in the world.

### The Jews Respond (Dan. 3:16–18)

Shadrach, Meshach, and Abednego refused to compromise. They knew their God was able to save them (**the God we serve is able to save us**, v. 17), but they also knew there were no guarantees (**but even if he does not**, v. 18). That is to say, their honoring of God was not conditional upon His preserving them from the fire. So either way, whether the men were saved or incinerated, Nebuchadnezzar lost.

---

### WORDS FROM WESLEY

*Daniel 3:18*

*But if not*—It was therefore all one to them, which way God would honour himself; they were resolved to suffer rather than sin, and leave the cause to God. Indeed if God be for us, we need not fear what man can do unto us. Let him do his worst. God will deliver us either from death, or in death. (ENOT)

---

### Death by Burning in the Furnace (Dan. 3:19–23)

Enough was enough for Nebuchadnezzar. Interestingly, the Aramaic word for *attitude* in the expression **his attitude toward them changed** (v. 19) is exactly the same as the one for "image" (of gold) in verse 1. There is a certain image of gold and a certain image on Nebuchadnezzar's face.

Like Isaac, who was bound and placed on the altar's fire (Gen. 22:9), the three Jews **were bound and thrown into the blazing furnace** (v. 21). But in both cases, divine intervention prevented the loss of life. To further emphasize the miraculous nature of God's deliverance, we are told that the **furnace** was **so hot that the flames of the fire killed the soldiers** (v. 22) who threw the three in. If those outside the furnace were slain by its heat, what chance of surviving did those inside the furnace have?

---

### WORDS FROM WESLEY
*Daniel 3:23*

*Fell down*—All this is exprest with emphasis, to make the power of God more glorious in their preservation; for that shame that slew the executioners, might much more easily have killed them, even before they fell down. (ENOT)

---

### God Rescues Those Who Honor Him (Dan. 3:24–28)

There is no deliverance *from* the fire, but there is deliverance *in* the fire. The three Jews were like the burning bush Moses saw (Ex. 3). They were in the fire, but they were not consumed by the fire. There was not even the **smell of fire on them** (v. 27).

And the reason is because of a **fourth** (v. 25) man in the fire, one whom Nebuchadnezzar identified as one who **looks like a son of the gods**. Perhaps **son of the gods** could be read as "a divine being." But who was this fourth person? God himself in recognizable form and shape? The angel of the Lord who earlier guided and protected Israel in the wilderness (Ex. 14:19) or helped Elijah in his time of crisis (1 Kings 19:7)? Or maybe an Old Testament manifestation of Christ?

---

### WORDS FROM WESLEY

*Daniel 3:25*

*No hurt*—See how the God of nature can when He pleases control the powers of nature! *The Son of God*—Probably He had heard Daniel speak of Him. Jesus Christ, the angel of the covenant, did sometimes appear before His incarnation. Those who suffer for Christ, have His gracious presence with them in their sufferings, even in the fiery furnace, even in the valley of the shadow of death, and therefore need fear no evil. (ENOT)

---

Nebuchadnezzar told the three Jews to **come out** (v. 26) of the furnace (through the lower door). Interestingly, when Shadrach, Meshach, and Abednego emerged from the furnace, they said absolutely nothing. There were no shouts of hallelujah, no glowing testimonies by them about the preserving and protecting grace of God. One wonders if this trio talked about this miracle for the rest of their lives, or not.

Nebuchadnezzar, on the other hand, could not restrain himself. While carefully screening out his own involvement in this brush-with-death episode, he offered this doxology: **"Praise be to the God . . . who has sent his angel and rescued his servants!"** (v. 28). Then he talked about the three Jews: **"They trusted in him** [God] **and defied the king's command and were willing to give up their lives rather than serve or worship any god except their own God."** Both the God of the Jews and the fierce loyalty of the Jews to their God have left an indelible impression on him. It was the Babylonian king, not the three Jews, who was changed by this ordeal.

## DISCUSSION

Share about a time when your faith was challenged, questioned by others, or ridiculed.

1. Daniel faced penalties for his refusal to worship an idol. While few in our culture worship statues, what are some false gods that capture people's attention?

2. What were the circumstances in Daniel's life at the time of this incident? How might those circumstances have affected his choices?

3. Many Christians have faced persecution or martyrdom. What do you think makes a person willing to die for the faith?

4. If the three men had perished in the fire, would their faith have been in vain? Explain why you think as you do.

5. Do you think persecution of Christians could occur in our society?

6. What issue in our society might require Christians to take a stand for their faith?

7. If your faith is not tested in some way (as Daniel's was), how would you know how strong it is?

8. What actions, habits, or activities would serve to strengthen your faith?

9. What might you do to support or encourage Christians who are being persecuted for their faith?

## PRAYER

Father, help us to stand for You lest we fall for anything else.

**12**

# FROM PRIDE TO HUMILITY

*Daniel 4:28–37*

---

Pride results in judgment, but God restores the humble.

Pride is an insidious form of sin. Devilishly difficult to see in ourselves (yet somehow easily recognized in others), it is the underlying attitude that fuels much of our wrong behavior. Gossip, greed, revenge, slander, and adultery may all have their roots in that most hungry creature, the human ego. Our desire to place ourselves and our needs ahead of others is the root of all kinds of mischief.

While prideful behavior may be tolerated—and even celebrated—in our achievement-oriented, celebrity-driven culture, God takes the sin of pride most seriously. This study will cause you to examine your heart for evidence of this creeping sin and to think rightly of yourself in relationship to God and others.

## COMMENTARY

This is the fourth and final incident from the life of Nebuchadnezzar recorded in Daniel.

The arrangement of this fourth chapter is deliberately and skillfully done. While verses 4–27 and 34–37 are written in the first person, verses 28–33 are cast in the third person. The intended effect of this is clear. Verses 28–33 detail Nebuchadnezzar's madness and obviously, given such a malady, the king would not have been able to write of it himself. Someone else would need to do that. Even though the writer could have continued in the first person for these verses, he deliberately chose not to do so.

The effective design of this chapter is indicative of the writer's skill.

Regardless of the writer's skill, however, the reader's focus is likely to center on the credibility of this event. Both the king's malady and conversion are difficult to accept. Babylonian palace records contain no reference either to his absence from the throne or his apparent conversion.

There are two extrabiblical references to Nebuchadnezzar's animal-like existence. Eusebius of Caesarea (A.D. 265–339) makes reference to Nebuchadnezzar's illness. However, it is fourth-hand information and thus perhaps should not be given too much weight. There is an earlier reference by Josephus (A.D. 37–?) to Nebuchadnezzar's illness in conjunction with his building program in Babylon. At least in these sources there is some evidence of Nebuchadnezzar's illness, even of its psychological nature.

Nebuchadnezzar was the most important king of the Neo-Babylonian Empire. His reign of over four decades (605–562 B.C.) is relatively well documented. There are no hints of a hiatus in his reign or of any abnormal behavior. Certainly there is no record of a life-changing conversion.

But the official annals (*The Babylonian Chronicles*) end with the eleventh year of his reign (594 B.C.). Information dealing with the last thirty years of his reign is quite limited. But even if there were palace records of these particular years, perhaps one would not expect to find this humiliation recorded.

Even apart from the issue of historical collaboration of this biblical passage, the strangeness of this illness is difficult to explain.

One, of course, could quickly dismiss this account, classifying it as a tale. But even many critics are slow to do this. Three explanations of the king's malady have been advanced.

Some characterize Nebuchadnezzar's malady as possibly as being lycanthropy, an illness rather well attested in prescientific times. As such it is linked with hydrophobia, rabies. The sufferer apparently retains his consciousness in other respects but thinks himself changed into some animal and thus behaves in the manner of that animal. While most frequently the animals imitated were dogs and wolves, here in this passage it is the ox Nebuchadnezzar imitated—perhaps a kind of boanthropy. The diagnostic decline of lycanthropy is said to be due to a more widespread recognition of psychological disorders and better care for the afflicted person.

Others suggest this illness was transferred from the lesser known King Nabonidus to the better known Nebuchadnezzar. Nabonidus was king of Babylon shortly after Nebuchadnezzar (556–539 B.C.). While he is not directly referred to in Daniel, his son, Belshazzar, functioning as a regent, is the king associated with the handwriting on the wall. Nabonidus's absence was the reason for Belshazzar's regency. Nabonidus was in Teima of Arabia. He was out of favor with the priests of Babylon since he did not give due preference to the god Marduk. At best he was regarded as highly unusual and eccentric, at worse, insane.

A more figurative approach notes the role animals play in Daniel. Animals are used in Daniel 7 to designate various empires—all of which are disposed by the Son of Man. Further Scripture recognizes a human inclination to animality. Humans degenerate to the level of animals when God is forgotten.

While details of this chapter are difficult, its meaning is clear and it is for this reason that it is included in Scripture. This narrative, as the other three, emphasizes that God is greater than any human potentate and that power exercised by a king has been conferred by God. God can choose to use the king—in this case Nebuchadnezzar—to achieve His purposes, as in Jeremiah, where power and authority were given to Nebuchadnezzar to effect the destruction of Jerusalem and thereby punish Judah, or He can dispose and humble a king as here in Daniel 4.

A common theme in Scripture is that God will not tolerate hubris. Such was the case with Saul, who lost the kingship through arrogance (1 Sam. 13:13–14), and David, who brought a pestilence upon the nation for the same reason (1 Chron. 21:1–27). In the New Testament Herod Agrippa I is also guilty of pride. Of him we read: "Herod . . . delivered a public address to the people. They shouted, 'This is the voice of a god, not of a man.' Immediately, because Herod did not give praise to God, an angel of the Lord struck him down, and he was eaten by worms and died" (Acts 12:21–23).

Rulers, by reason of their opportunities for exercising power, are more severely tempted to forget their status as creatures. They may consider themselves sovereign, but they are not. Hubris can only lead to a fall.

### Dream Fulfilled (Dan. 4:28–33)

**All this happened to King Nebuchadnezzar** (v. 28). This verse anticipates what follows and introduces us to the climax of this narrative. The writer is not so much concerned with what happened but rather that it was the fulfillment of God's word.

**Twelve months later** (v. 29) indicates that a year passed after the interpretation of the dream before the onset of the illness. Perhaps this can be seen as a time for Nebuchadnezzar to repent and change his ways, thus reflecting the mercy and patience of God. Daniel, at the time of interpreting the dream, had counseled Nebuchadnezzar with the following words: "Renounce your sins by doing what is right, and your wickedness by being kind to the oppressed. It may be that then your prosperity will continue" (v. 27). But such went unheeded.

**As the king was walking on the roof of the royal palace** (v. 29), Nebuchadnezzar made the boast that led to his downfall. The roof of a palace was an ordinary place for a king to walk. From such a vantage point he could gaze out over his city. It was while walking on the roof of the palace that David observed Bathsheba (2 Sam. 11:2), resulting in activities severely condemned by the prophet Nathan.

Nebuchadnezzar's characterization of Babylon as **great** (Dan. 4:30) was not simply imaginative. Babylon was indeed a magnificent city. Nebuchadnezzar was better known as a builder than a conqueror, and he took pride in that. Babylon is described to be 3.2 square miles in size, straddling the Euphrates River, with inner walls twenty-one feet thick, and towers thirty to sixty feet high occurring every sixty feet. Not only was it large, but, it was known for its opulence as well. Temples to Marduk and some fifty other gods adorned the city, along with statues of more than two hundred other divinities. The glory of Babylon was such that John, in Revelation 18, used it to refer to the grandeur—as well as the sin—of the Rome of his day.

But the issue was not Babylon's magnificence. Rather it was Nebuchadnezzar's taking credit for it. Note his words: **"Is not this the great Babylon I have built as the royal residence, by my mighty power and for the glory of my majesty?"** (Dan. 4:30). Such an egotistical claim left God out of his reckoning and also the many oppressed laborers who did the actual work. His assertion becomes even more offensive, for he claimed not only was the city built *by* him but it was also built *for* him! The city existed to bring fame and notoriety to him. Such egotistical words are in keeping with what we know of Nebuchadnezzar.

As Nebuchadnezzar bragged about his accomplishments, his words stuck in his throat. His boasting was interrupted by a **voice ... from heaven** (v. 31) that repeated Daniel's warning (v. 25) with a critical modification. The phrase **your royal authority has been taken from you** is added. Daniel at best could only warn. It is God who gives authority to human potentates and removes it from them. Through Jeremiah God said, "I will hand all your countries over to my servant Nebuchadnezzar king of Babylon" (Jer. 27:6). Now He removed them from the king's jurisdiction.

The grace period of twelve months had not changed Nebuchadnezzar. At the end of that period, **immediately what had been said about Nebuchadnezzar was fulfilled** (Dan. 4:33).

The length of this illness hangs on the expression **seven times will pass by for you** (v. 32), generally understood to mean seven years—a rather extended illness. The details—**until his hair grew like the feathers of an eagle and his nails like the claws of a bird** (v. 33)—are added to Daniel's earlier description of his condition in verse 23.

### Ascription of Praise (Dan. 4:34–37)

While the text indicates that **at the end of that time** Nebuchadnezzar's **sanity was restored** (v. 34), it should not be seen as an automatic cure. The phrase **raised my eyes toward heaven** indicates his acknowledgement of God's sovereignty and his looking to God for help. Animal behavior was now replaced by human behavior, which allowed for a response to God.

---

### WORDS FROM WESLEY
#### Daniel 4:34

*Mine understanding returned*—God shined upon his soul, and gave him understanding to consider his sad state, and the causes of it. *And honoured him*—By prayer and praise, adoring the justice and mercy of God, giving God the glory of His sovereignty and unchangeableness. (ENOT)

---

**The Most High** (v. 34) and **the King of heaven** (v. 37) are designations used by Nebuchadnezzar of God. The former can be found earlier in this chapter (v. 2), while the latter is a unique designation for God in the Bible. Heaven is used as a synonym for God in this chapter (vv. 13, 20, 26, 39). Nebuchadnezzar acknowledged that God's **dominion is an eternal dominion; his kingdom endures from generation to generation** (v. 34). Not only is this sovereignty exercised **with the powers of heaven** but among **the peoples of the earth** (v. 35) as well.

## WORDS FROM WESLEY

### Daniel 4:35

*As nothing*—A due consideration of God's infinite greatness, makes the creature appear as nothing; creatures are nothing to help, nothing to hurt, nothing in duration, nothing solid and substantial nothing without dependence, and influence, and support from God. *His will*—Being the Lord of hosts, and the only absolute and universal monarch of the world. (ENOT)

Nebuchadnezzar's return to sanity led to the restoration of his **honor and splendor** and to the return of his **advisors and nobles** (v. 36). Not only was it **restored** but he asserted he **became even greater than before**. Such a statement may indicate that any alleged change in Nebuchadnezzar was no more real and vital than it was in the previous chapters. He had been returned to humanness, but had his hubris been effectively handled? Perhaps Nebuchadnezzar's response was a confessional acknowledgment without any significant commitment. It would appear to fall short of true faith.

## WORDS FROM WESLEY

### Daniel 4:37

*Now I praise*—Thus can the Lord make the stoutest hearts to stoop, and do Him homage. This doxology proceeds from his heart. *Are truth*—God is truth essentially: He is the rule and standard of truth, His words are truth, His ways are truth, and they are judgment: He is wise, and hath dealt justly with me for my pride, and in very faithfulness hath afflicted me, and in very tenderness hath restored me; I do, and ever shall adore Him for it. *Able to abase*—As He hath declared upon me, in stupendous changes, which I proclaim to all the world. He had a just controversy with me, and I have no ground to quarrel with Him, but to give Him glory by this confession. What authority had any one to say, That this man "was no convert?" We can no more doubt of his salvation than of Solomon's. (ENOT)

Finally, note there is no indictment of God, no challenge to His truth and justice. The king singles out these two appropriate characteristics of God, but they are not abstracted. God was truthful in that He did as promised, and just in that Nebuchadnezzar sinned by failing to heed Daniel's warning. The theme of this study is caught in the words **those who walk in pride he is able to humble** (v. 37).

---

### WORDS FROM WESLEY

*Daniel 4:37*

Throughout my fallen soul I feel
The strength of pride invincible;
But Thou, the' almighty God of grace,
Canst proud aspiring worms abase:
All things are possible to Thee,
Display Thy humbling power on me,
And for His sake, to me impart
My Saviour's lowliness of heart. (PW, vol. 10, 69)

## DISCUSSION

Explain why it is unreasonable to think that a powerful person could also be humble.

1. What factors may have contributed to Nebuchadnezzar's pride?

2. Nebuchadnezzar was humbled by mental illness. What kinds of circumstances might humble a person today?

3. If one aspect of pride is an obsession with self, list some symptoms of pride that may be commonly accepted in our culture.

4. How would you define *humility*?

5. Think of a humble person you know. How does his or her example affect you?

6. How would you react if a close, trusted friend pointed out pride in you?

7. If you realized you had just one year to live, what would be your highest priorities?

## PRAYER

Lord, help us to see ourselves neither too positively nor too negatively but exactly as You see us.

# 13

# ENDURING CONFLICT FAITHFULLY

*Daniel 6:10–23*

We endure persecution by entrusting ourselves to God.

The persecution of Christians, though seldom seen in North America, is a fact of life in many parts of the world. Given the rising influence of Islam across the globe, some predict that persecution will become more widespread in years to come. If your faith were challenged by the threat of violence, how would you respond? Do you feel certain enough of what you believe to risk losing your home, your family, or your life?

This study is a reminder that persecution can come at any time, even after many years of religious toleration and peace. This study of Daniel's life will give you confidence to stand for what you believe, regardless of the circumstances.

## COMMENTARY

Daniel was a Hebrew, having been taken to Babylon as a young man by king Nebuchadnezzar when he conquered Judah. Daniel was a pious youth, and along with three of his friends, refused to defile himself with the delicacies of the king's table. As a result, God honored him and he was eventually elevated to the status of the second ruler over the entire kingdom. Even with the rise and fall of different rulers over Babylon and Persia (Nebuchadnezzar, Belshazzar, Darius), Daniel remained in a position of prominence. In addition to his capable administration of government, Daniel was also known for his dreams and his interpretation of the dreams of the kings.

The book of Daniel is attributed by conservative scholars to Daniel and covers the time period of 604–534 B.C. Although a number of contemporary critics discredit its authenticity, Jesus himself gave it His full endorsement as He quoted from it on a number of occasions.

Chapter 6 records that in Daniel's later life, during the reign of Darius the Mede, Daniel was appointed as one of three administrators to oversee the rule of one hundred twenty appointed satraps (vv. 1–2). He distinguished himself so highly in this capacity that King Darius planned to set Daniel over the whole kingdom (v. 3). This caused the administrators and satraps to attempt to find charges they could bring against Daniel in his conduct of government affairs, but they were unable to do so (v. 4). Because Daniel was a man of great trustworthiness and integrity, there was no evidence of corruption or negligence. He was also a man of great devotion to the God of Israel. Eventually his enemies realized that the only way they were going to succeed in putting Daniel in disfavor with the king was to trap him in some act of defiance to Babylonian worship (v. 5). So they concocted a scheme whereby the king would issue a decree that would declare that no one in the kingdom could pray to any god or king except Darius for thirty days. That decree forms the backdrop of this text.

### Daniel's Devotion to God (Dan. 6:10–11)

It didn't take long for Daniel to learn of the decree of Darius. And if he had obeyed this decree, it would have seriously altered his devotional habits. But his loyalty to the God of heaven superseded any loyalty he had to an earthly ruler. So **he went home to his upstairs room where the windows opened toward Jerusalem** (v. 10), and he began to pray. It was not deliberate, open defiance of the king. This was simply his pattern. Three times a day he was accustomed to humbling himself before God by getting on his knees. Three times a day he opened his windows toward Jerusalem, a practice that was common among the exiles at that time. Three times a day he gave thanks to God. His enemies knew that. They counted on it. That's why they tricked Darius into signing the decree—it was the only way they knew to catch Daniel in an act of disobedience to the law.

---

## WORDS FROM WESLEY

### *Daniel 6:10*

*Toward Jerusalem*—The temple was the place where the Lord placed His name, and promised to appear, and accept His people, all being a type of Christ, through whom only sinners are accepted. *As he did aforetime*—He did not abate his prayers for the king's command, nor did he break the law purposely, because he did no more than he was wont to do in serving his God. (ENOT)

---

Anyone else might have been tempted to simply put this area of life on hold for thirty days until the order was over, but Daniel knew how critical prayer was to his daily life. Daniel knew he needed to spend time in prayer if he was going to have any power in the ordeal that awaited him. Like Elijah, Daniel had discovered that "the prayer of a righteous man is powerful and effective" (James 5:16). Daniel's prayer life is well documented throughout the book. In 2:17, we find him praying corporately with his three friends concerning the Lord's assistance in interpreting Nebuchadnezzar's dream. In 6:10, we find him praying privately. In 9:3 (and throughout the whole chapter), we find him praying earnestly. In 10:2–3, he prayed desperately. And in the Lord's answer to him in 10:12, we find an indication that he prayed powerfully as well.

So when Daniel's adversaries went to his home to check on him, they found exactly what they expected. They **went as a**

**group and found Daniel praying and asking God for help** (v. 11). And God is more than willing to give His help to us if we will only seek, ask, and knock. Undoubtedly Daniel was mindful of Psalm 91 as he prayed. "He who dwells in the shelter of the Most High will rest in the shadow of the Almighty. I will say of the LORD, 'He is my refuge and my fortress, my God, in whom I trust.' . . . For he will command his angels concerning you to guard you in all your ways . . . you will trample the great lion and the serpent. 'Because he loves me,' says the LORD, 'I will protect him, for he acknowledges my name. He will call upon me, and I will answer him; I will be with him in trouble, I will deliver him and honor him.'"

## The King's Decree (Dan. 6:12–15)

When they discovered Daniel at prayer, his adversaries went immediately to King Darius with a report of what they had found. First, they reminded him of the royal decree they had convinced him to sign. They had originally convinced Darius that this edict had the full support of all of the king's administrators, including Daniel (v. 7), but this was obviously a lie. Consequently, with his ego stroked by their cunning flattery, Darius had signed the order.

Now, having procured the evidence they desired, they announced to the king, **"Daniel, who is one of the exiles from Judah, pays no attention to you, O king, or to the decree you put in writing"** (v. 13). They had successfully trapped him. Even though Daniel was a loyal subject and faithful servant of Darius, he had in fact gone against the king's written edict. And with that transgression also came the inordinate consequence of being thrown into a lions' den.

Christians around the world are faced with similar laws today. Some find themselves in countries that seek to enforce Islamic or Hindu rule and make it illegal to worship any other god but their own. Some find themselves in countries where they must either register their church or Bible study with the state or risk arrest. Others live in countries where conversion is punishable by death. Darius's edict sounds ominously familiar to many believers around the world today.

Darius became **greatly distressed** (v. 14). Even though he knew Daniel was guilty of transgressing his edict, he also knew in his heart that Daniel was a faithful administrator and even a friend. He certainly did not deserve the harsh penalty of being thrown into a den of lions, no matter how many times a day he prayed to his God. So Darius became **determined to rescue Daniel and made every effort until sundown to save him.**

But Daniel's adversaries would not let either Daniel or Darius off the hook. There was a code in the law of the Medes and Persians that said, in effect, no decree or edict the king issued could be changed. Once it was signed and published, it could not be rescinded. So Darius was stuck. He had to follow through with the order, even though he now understood how absurd it really was and how these men had manipulated him in their plan to get rid of Daniel. It certainly looked like they had won.

## The Lord's Protection (Dan. 6:16–23)

Reluctantly, King Darius gave the order and Daniel was rounded up and thrown into a lions' den. It was fairly common for Babylonian and Persian kings to keep lions around their palaces in large cistern-like pits. They were symbolic of strength and royalty, and their ferocity was a reminder of the king's ultimate power over his enemies. But Daniel was hardly an enemy. And at eighty-two years of age, he was certainly no physical match against a lion, let alone a cistern full of hungry ones. Just the simple fall from being thrown into the pit would have been dangerous enough to his health.

One of the touching points of this story is the concern, and possibly even the faith of King Darius, concerning Daniel's plight. He told him, **"May your God, whom you serve continually, rescue you!"** (v. 16). Daniel's faith in God was no secret to the king. He had been open about it from the very beginning of his sojourn in Babylon. His faith had already sustained him and his companions through several trying situations, but now the king hoped Daniel's faith would somehow sustain him through this ordeal as well.

---

### WORDS FROM WESLEY

*Daniel 6:20*

*Able to deliver*—What he doubted of, we are sure of, that the servants of the living God, have a master who is able to deliver them, and bear them out in His service. (ENOT)

---

Nevertheless, Darius had a stone brought and placed over the mouth of the den so Daniel could not escape. Then he and his nobles sealed it with imprints of their own rings so that no one (including the king himself) would come to Daniel's rescue. There was no human way of escape! And the king knew it well, for when he returned to his palace he couldn't eat, he couldn't sleep, and he couldn't even be distracted by his usual entertainments. He could only worry and wait until morning.

**At the first light of dawn, the king got up and hurried to the lions' den** (v. 19). He was anxious, but still hopeful. In fact, before he even got there he cried out to Daniel **in an anguished voice** (v. 20), inquiring as to whether his God had in fact rescued him from the mouths of the lions. To his pleasant surprise Daniel answered him and reported the tremendous miracle that had taken place. **God** had **sent his angel, and he shut the mouths of the lions** (v. 22). And why shouldn't He? Nothing is impossible for God. Throughout Daniel's life, God had shown him that no power is too great that He cannot stop it. No wisdom is too lofty that He cannot confound it. And no king is too high that he cannot be brought down.

---

### WORDS FROM WESLEY
#### *Daniel 6:22*

*His angel*—The same that was with the three children in the fiery furnace, whose presence made even the lions' den a strong-hold, His palace, His paradise. See the power of God over the fiercest creatures! See the care God takes of His faithful servants, especially when they are called to suffer for Him! See how ready the angels are to minister to the heirs of salvation! (ENOT)

---

Daniel told the king the reason God had done this thing for him—it was because God had found him innocent in His sight, and because he had never done any wrong before the king. His character and integrity were his defense. So the king, overjoyed at this point, had him lifted out of the lions' den. And when Daniel was inspected, no wound was found on him—not even a scratch from the fall! Daniel was rescued **because he had trusted in his God** (v. 23).

God honors the faith of His servants. And Hebrews 11 records the exploits of men and women who, through faith, "shut the mouths of lions, quenched the fury of the flames, and escaped the edge of the sword" (Heb. 11:33–34). But Hebrews 11 also reminds us that there were others who had similar faith and were chained and put in prison, stoned, put to death by the sword, even sawed in two (vv. 36–38). Was their faith inadequate? Didn't they trust God enough? The fact is, their faith was just as strong if not stronger than the others. But it looked beyond the present to the glory that would ultimately be theirs when they got to heaven. Sometimes God's higher purpose is actually served in the death of His faithful servants. But for Daniel, His purpose was to rescue him as a testimony of His power to save.

## WORDS FROM WESLEY

*Daniel 6:22*

How many times have we been strangely and unaccountably preserved, in sudden and dangerous falls! And it is well if we did not impute that preservation to chance, or to our own wisdom or strength. Not so: It was God gave His angels charge over us, and in their hands they bore us up. Indeed, men of the world will always impute such deliverances to accident or second causes. To these, possibly, some of them might have imputed Daniel's preservation in the lions' den. But himself ascribes it to the true cause: "My God hath sent his angel, and shut the lions' mouths" (Dan. 6:22).

When a violent disease, supposed incurable, is totally and suddenly removed, it is by no means improbable that this is effected by the ministry of an angel. And perhaps it is owing to the same cause, that a remedy is unaccountably suggested either to the sick person, or some attending upon him, by which he is entirely cured. (WJW, vol. 6, 367)

## DISCUSSION

Share about a time when you were accused of something you didn't do.

1. Describe Daniel's circumstances at the beginning of this story.

2. Contrast the character of Daniel with the character of his enemies.

3. The plan of Daniel's accusers backfired on them. Describe an instance you've seen in which a person's integrity enabled him or her to withstand attack.

4. What kinds of circumstances might Christians face today that would test their character?

5. Would you say that a silent witness, such as Daniel's, is necessarily better than a confrontational approach to critics? Why or why not?

6. What would enable you to stand firm during a test of faith?

7. Define what it means to have a clear conscience.

8. Daniel's faithfulness in prayer was used as a point of attack by enemies. At what point in your life might you be vulnerable— your marriage, your finances, your career, or something else?

9. How is it possible to create a meaningful prayer life when you are busy?

## PRAYER

Lord, keep us close to You, so that we may always hear Your voice clearly in times of trouble.

# WORDS FROM WESLEY WORKS CITED

ENOT: Wesley, J. (1765). *Explanatory Notes upon the Old Testament* (Vol. 1–3). Bristol: William Pine.

PW: *The Poetical Works of John and Charles Wesley.* Edited by D. D. G. Osborn. 13 vols. London: Wesleyan-Methodist Conference Office, 1868.

WJW: *The Works of John Wesley.* Third Edition, Complete and Unabridged. 14 vols. London: Wesleyan Methodist Book Room, 1872.

# OTHER BOOKS IN THE
# WESLEY BIBLE STUDIES SERIES

*Genesis*

*Exodus* (available April 2015)

*Leviticus through Deuteronomy* (available May 2015)

*Joshua through Ruth* (available May 2015)

*1 Samuel through 2 Chronicles*

*Ezra through Esther* (available April 2015)

*Job through Song of Songs*

*Isaiah* (available April 2015)

*Jeremiah through Daniel*

*Hosea through Malachi* (available May 2015)

*Matthew*

*Mark*

*Luke*

*John*

*Acts*

*Romans*

*1–2 Corinthians*

*Galatians through Colossians and Philemon*

*1–2 Thessalonians*

*1 Timothy through Titus*

*Hebrews*

*James*

*1–2 Peter and Jude*

*1–3 John*

*Revelation*

# Now Available in the Wesley Bible Studies Series

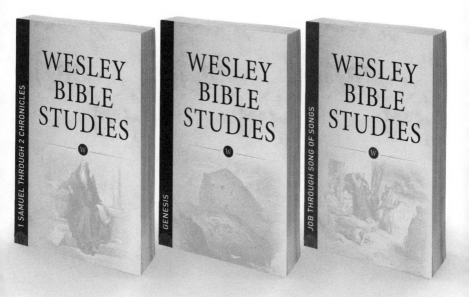

Each book in the Wesley Bible Studies series provides a thoughtful and powerful survey of key Scriptures in one or more biblical books. They combine accessible commentary from contemporary teachers, with relevantly highlighted direct quotes from the complete writings and life experiences of John Wesley, along with the poetry and hymns of his brother Charles. For each study, creative and engaging questions foster deeper fellowship and growth.

*1 Samuel through 2 Chronicles*
978-0-89827-866-8
978-0-89827-867-5 (e-book)

*Genesis*
978-0-89827-872-9
978-0-89827-873-6 (e-book)

*Job through Song of Songs*
978-0-89827-836-1
978-0-89827-837-8 (e-book)

1.800.493.7539  wphstore.com